Math Practice: Grades K–1

P9-CAF-798

Table of Contents

ISBN 978-1-60418-267-5
05-336131151

Ready-to-Use Ideas and Activities

The only way students truly will be able to manipulate numbers and have access to higher-level math concepts is to learn the basic tables and understand fundamental concepts, such as counting, addition, subtraction, time, fractions, measurement, shapes, and patterns.

The following activities can help to reinforce basic skills. These activities include a multi-sensory approach to helping students understand the concepts being introduced.

- Place a container filled with plastic discs near students' workspace. Plastic discs make great counters, which are extremely beneficial in helping students visualize mathematical concepts.

- Cut apart the flash cards provided in the back of this book. On small pieces of paper, write plus (+), minus (–), and equal (=) signs to use with the flash cards. Starting with a flash card that shows small numbers, put a flash card on a flat surface. Use the discs and the equation signs to show what is on the flash card. For example:

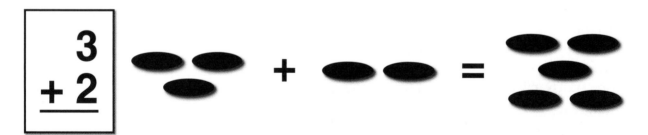

- Use the discs to show 3 + 2 = 5. After the discs are in place, have students state the problem and the answer aloud. Students can also do this in small groups.

- Use the discs to show examples of both addition and subtraction problems. After doing a number of examples using the flash cards, let students make up their own problems and show them visually using the discs.

CD-104317 • © Carson-Dellosa

Ready-to-Use Ideas and Activities

- Obtain a pair of dice and anything that can act as a three-minute timer (a timer, a stopwatch, a watch with a second hand, etc.), or decide upon a certain number of rounds of play. Have each student roll the dice and add the numbers showing on the faces. Each correct answer is worth one point. The student with the most correct answers after a specific period of time or number of rounds wins. For example, a game may consist of six rounds. The student with the most points after six rounds wins. Alternately, the game can be played with subtraction, subtracting the smaller number from the larger.

- As players memorize answers and gain confidence, add additional dice. When using more than two dice, have players state the problem aloud and answer as they go. For instance, if the dice show 3, 6, and 4, the player would say, "3 plus 6 is 9 and 9 plus 4 is 13."

- Create a bingo sheet with five rows and five columns of blank squares. Write *FREE* in the middle square. Make enough copies to give one to each student. Write the flash card problems on a chalkboard and have students choose 24 problems from the board to write in the empty spaces of their bingo cards.

- When students have finished filling out their bingo cards, make the flash cards into a deck. Call out the answers one at a time. If a student has a problem on his card that equals the called-out answer, he should make an X through the problem to cross it out. Allow only one problem per answer. The student who first crosses out five problems in a row—horizontally, vertically, or diagonally—wins the game when she shouts, "Bingo!"

- Play another fun version of this game by writing answers on the bingo sheet and calling out the problems. To extend the game, continue playing until a student crosses out all of the problems on his bingo sheet.

Name _____   Date _____

Counting 0–5

• •

Count each group of objects. Circle the correct number.

1	2	3	4	5

1	2	3	4	5

1	2	3	4	5

1	2	3	4	5

1	2	3	4	5

                                    CD-104317 • © Carson-Dellosa

Counting 0–5

Draw a line to match each basket to the correct number of eggs.

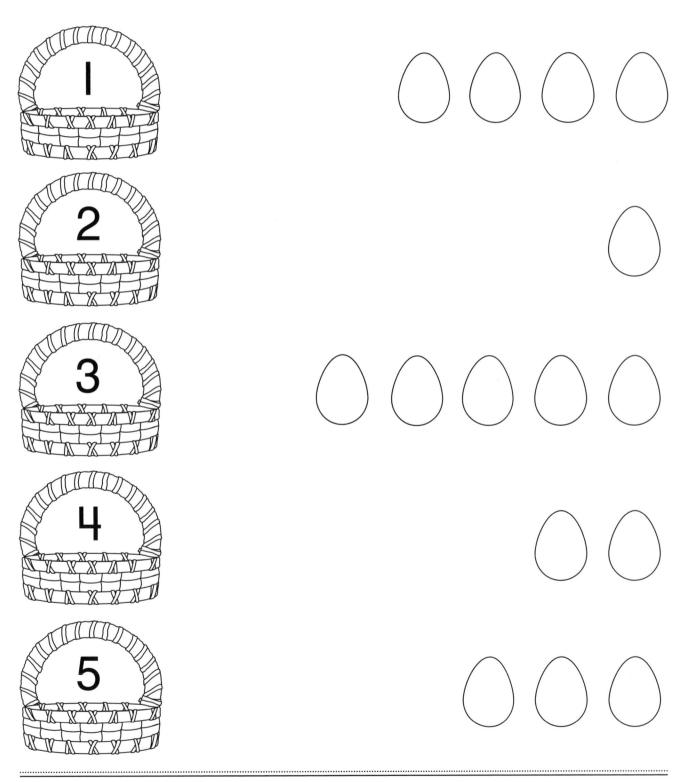

Counting 0–5

Count each group of objects. Write the correct number in each blank.

_____

_____

_____

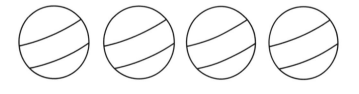

_____

_____

CD-104317 • © Carson-Dellosa

Counting 6–10

Count each group of objects. Circle the correct number.

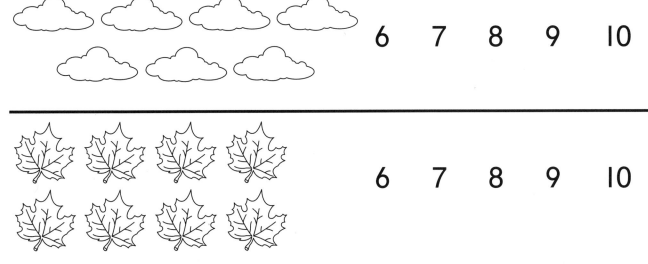

6   7   8   9   10

6   7   8   9   10

6   7   8   9   10

6   7   8   9   10

6   7   8   9   10

Counting 6–10

Draw a line to match each set of drawers to the correct number of shirts.

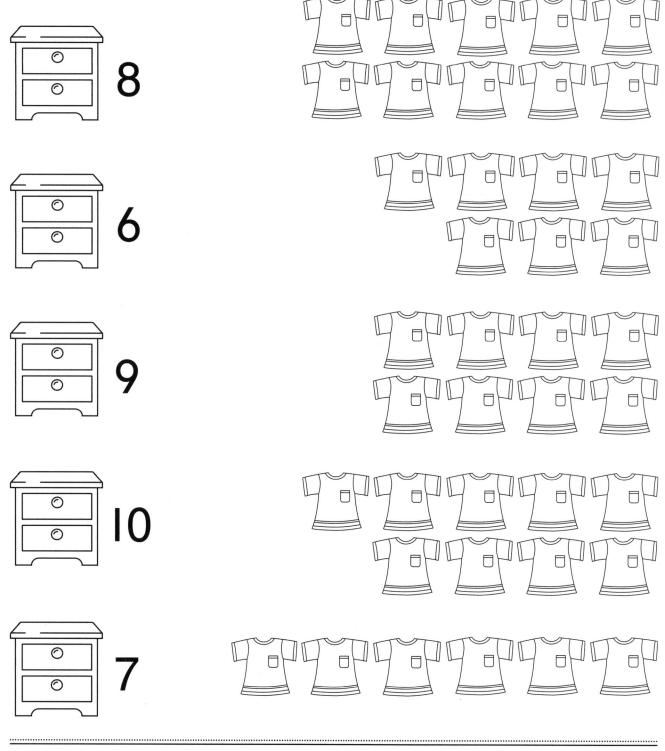

Counting 6–10

Count each group of objects. Write the correct number in each blank.

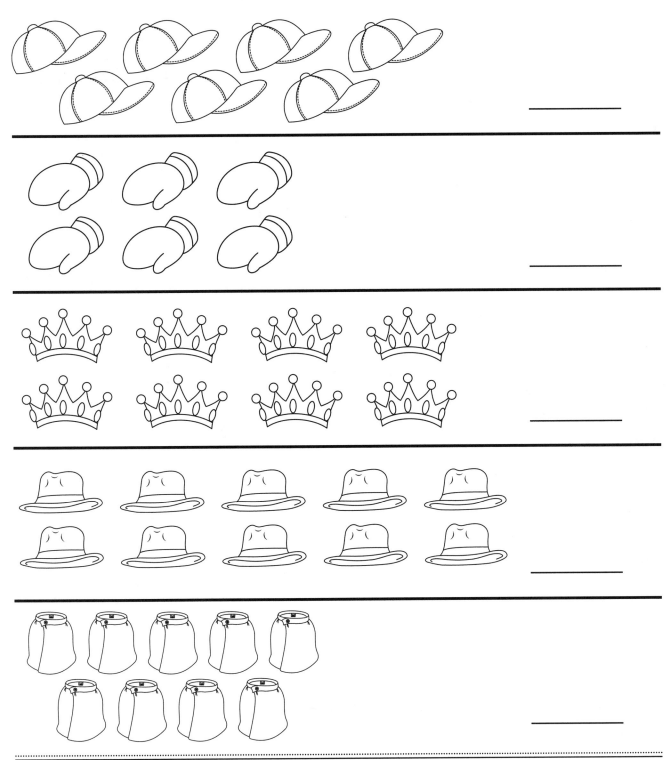

_____

_____

_____

_____

_____

Name _____   Date _____

Counting 11–15

Count each group of objects. Circle the correct number.

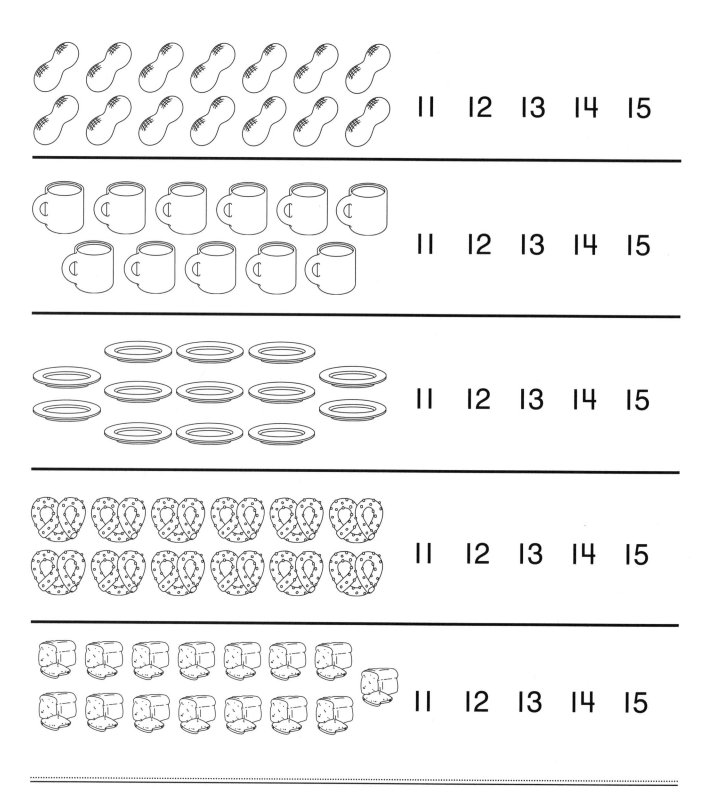

11   12   13   14   15

11   12   13   14   15

11   12   13   14   15

11   12   13   14   15

11   12   13   14   15

  CD-104317 • © Carson-Dellosa

Counting 11–15

Draw a line to match each vase to the correct number
of flowers.

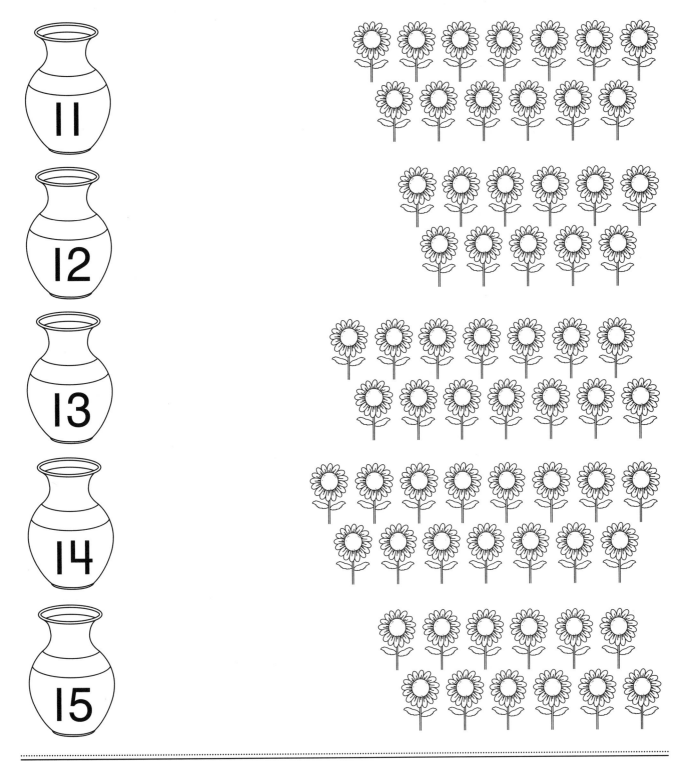

Counting 16–20

Count each group of shapes. Write the correct number in each blank.

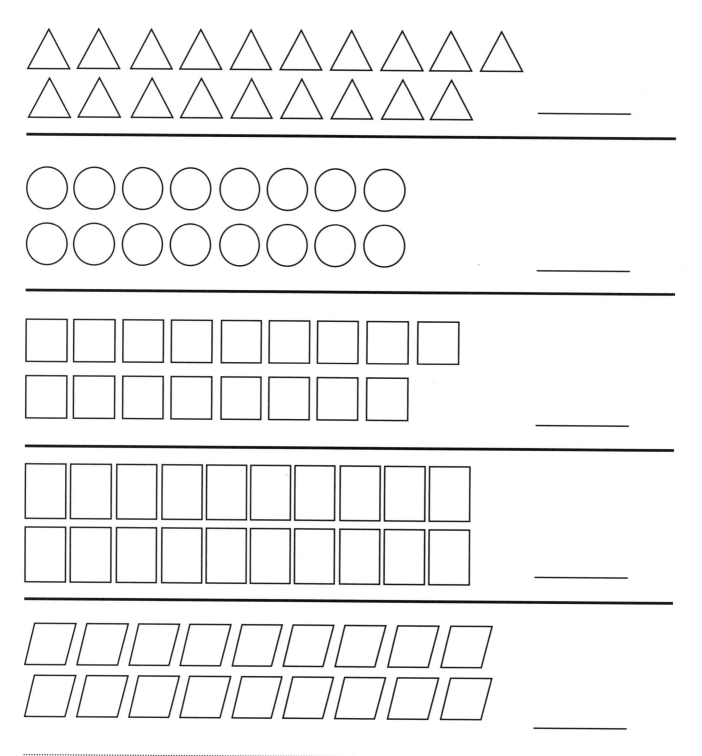

Numbers in a Sequence

Write the number that comes **next**.

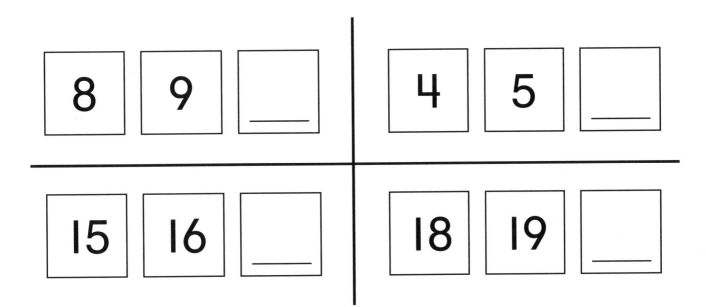

Write the number that comes **first**.

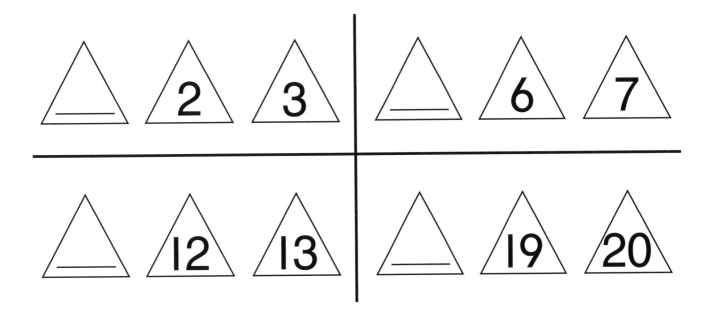

Numbers in a Sequence

Write the number that comes **between**.

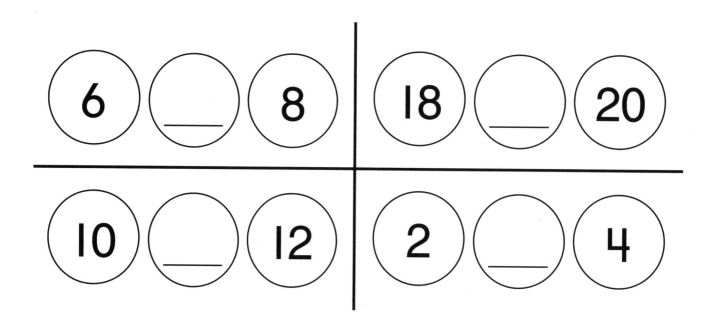

Write the missing number.

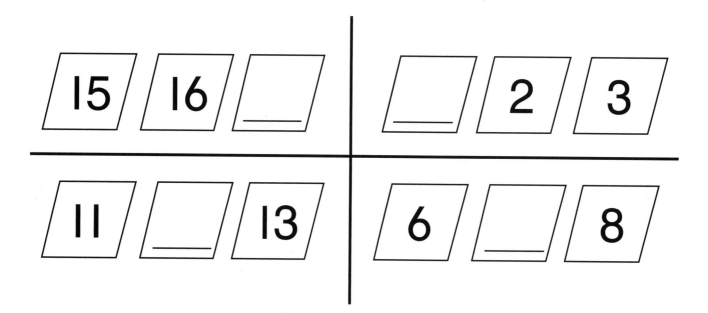

CD-104317 • © Carson-Dellosa

Comparing Numbers

Circle the **greater** number in each star.

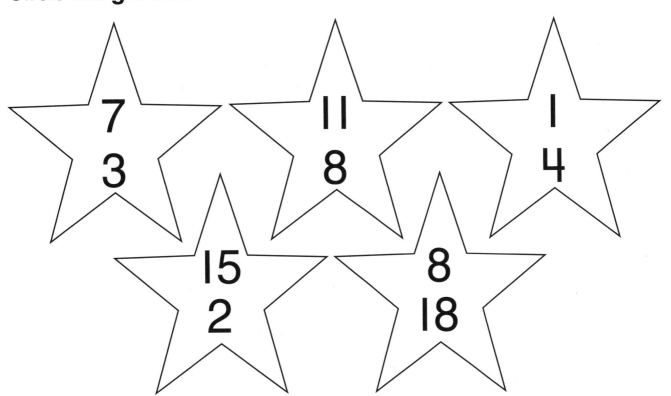

Circle the **lesser** number in each moon.

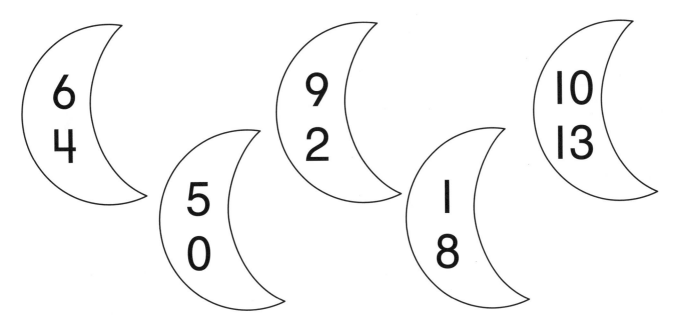

Comparing Groups

Circle the group with **more** objects.

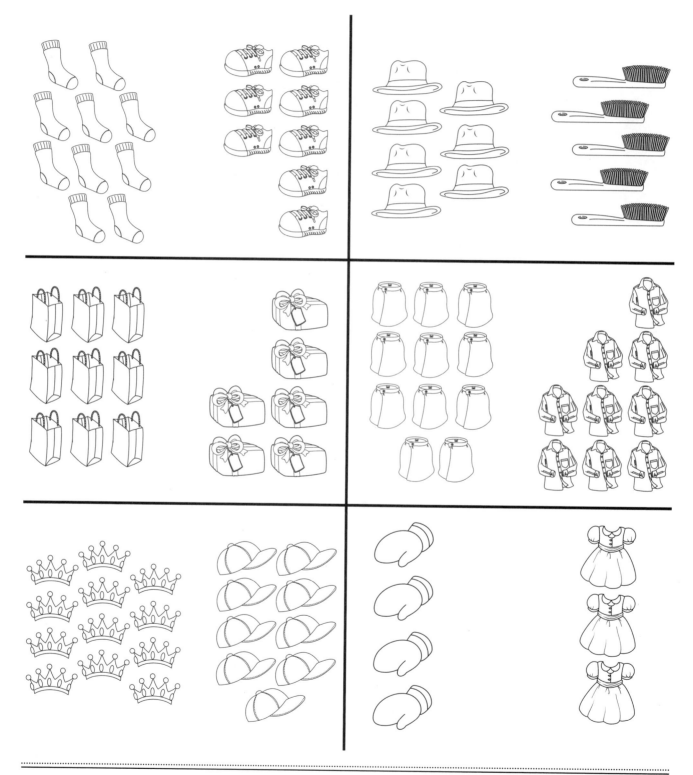

Comparing Groups

Circle the group with **more** objects.

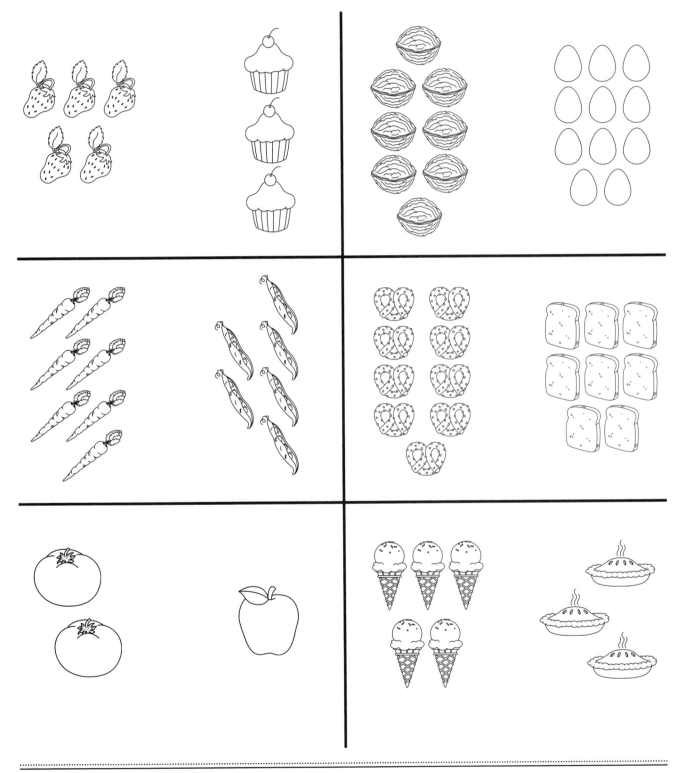

Comparing Groups

Circle the group with **less** objects.

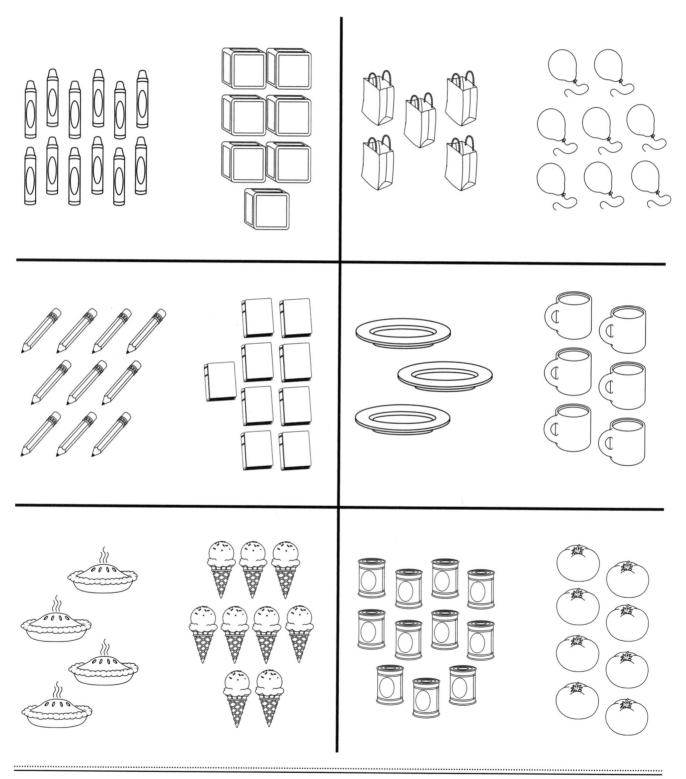

CD-104317 • © Carson-Dellosa

Matching Groups

· ·

Draw lines to match the groups that have the **same** number of objects.

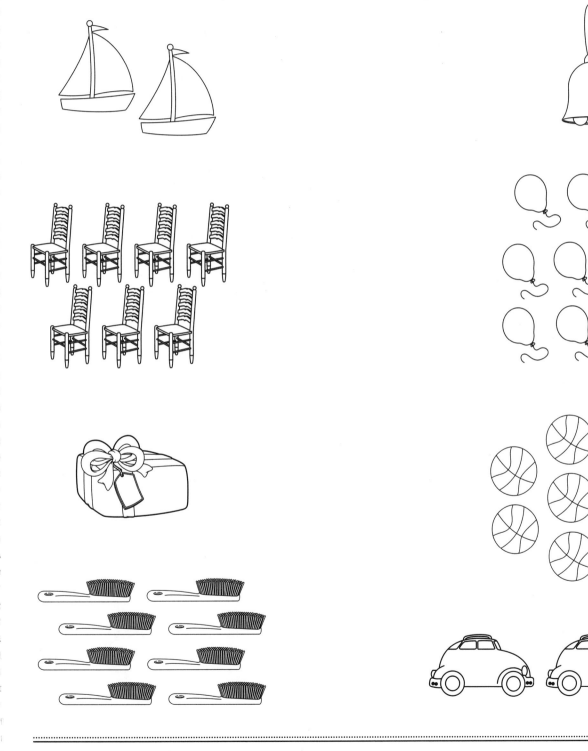

Name _____ Date _____

Matching Groups

Draw lines to match the groups that have the **same** number of objects.

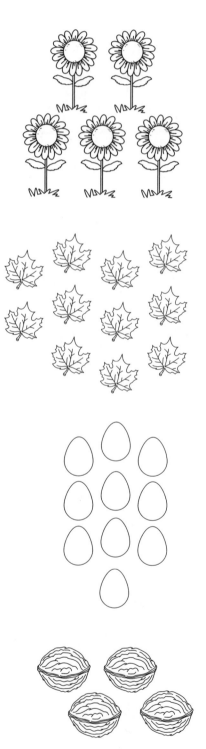

Number Words

· ·

Circle the correct number word.

	1	five nine one		2	ten two six
	3	three nine two		4	seven zero four
	5	two five eight		6	three ten six
	7	seven zero four		8	two zero eight
	9	nine six one		10	one eight ten

Number Words

• •

Draw a line to match each number to the correct number word.

11	fourteen
12	eleven
13	fifteen
14	twelve
15	thirteen

Number Words

• •

Draw a line to match each number to the correct number word.

16		nineteen
17		sixteen
18		twenty
19		seventeen
20		eighteen

Ordinal Numbers

• •

Circle the ordinal number that names the position of each item below.

1 first	2 second	3 third	4 fourth	5 fifth	6 sixth	7 seventh	8 eighth	9 ninth	10 tenth

(balloon)	first	sixth	fourth
(dress)	tenth	eighth	third
(shoe)	ninth	first	third
(bucket)	seventh	third	fifth
(pretzel)	sixth	first	second
(light bulb)	ninth	fourth	first
(bell)	fifth	seventh	ninth
(key)	first	ninth	fifth
(bone)	first	fifth	eighth
(ball)	third	seventh	ninth

CD-104317 • © Carson-Dellosa

Name _____ Date _____

Even Numbers

Numbers that end in 0, 2, 4, 6, or 8 are even numbers.
Even numbers can be divided into two equal groups.
Circle the **even numbers** in each row.

1	2	3	6	9
4	5	8	10	13
12	14	15	17	19
18	19	21	24	25
19	22	27	28	30
24	26	27	29	32

In each blank, write the **even number** that would come next.

2, 4, ___, 8, ___, 12, 14, 16, ___

Odd Numbers
· ·

Numbers that end in 1, 3, 5, 7, or 9 are odd numbers.
Odd numbers cannot be divided into two equal groups.
Circle the **odd numbers** in each row.

1	4	5	6	9
3	7	8	10	11
10	12	13	14	15
16	17	19	22	23
20	21	25	26	27
25	26	28	29	30

In each blank, write the **odd number** that would come next.

1, ___, 5, 7, 9, ___, 13, ___, 17

 CD-104317 • © Carson-Dellosa

Counting by 2s

On each number line, place a dot on the first even number.
Then, skip count by 2s. Place a dot on each number in
the pattern.

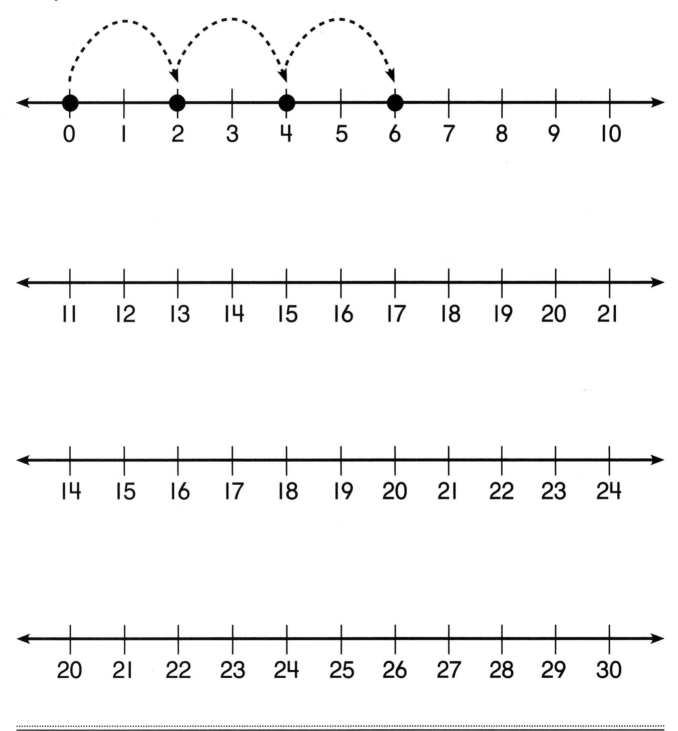

Counting by 2s

• •

Write the missing numbers. Skip count by 2s.

1		3		5
	7		9	
11		13		15
	17		19	

Continue the pattern from the grid above. Skip count by 2s. Fill in the blanks.

22 , _____ , _____ , _____ , _____

Name _____   Date _____

Counting by 2s

. . . .

Complete the pattern. Skip count by 2s.

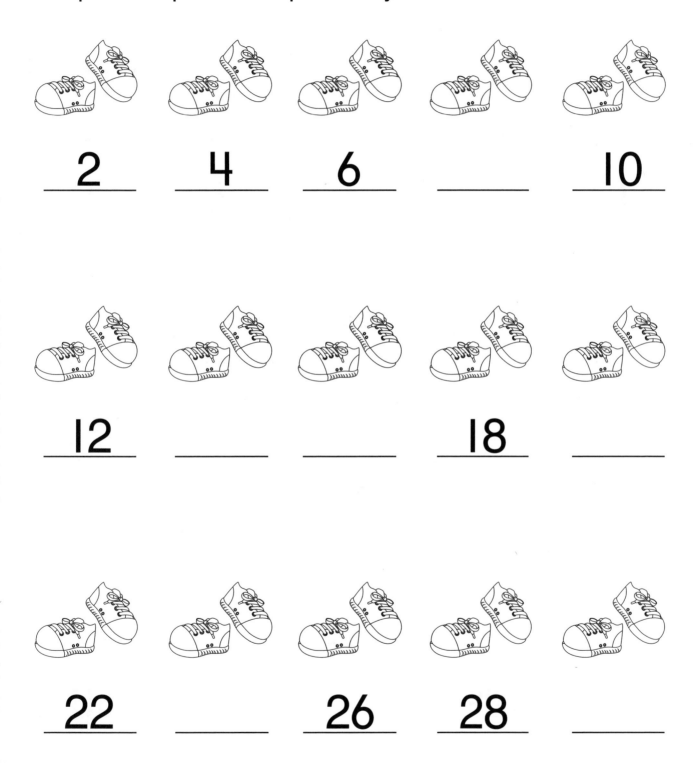

2   4   6   ____   10

12   ____   ____   18   ____

22   ____   26   28   ____

Counting by 2s

Write the missing numbers. Skip count by 2s.

2	4		8	10
12		16	18	20
	24	26		

		6	8	10
12	14		18	
22	24			30

Name _____ Date _____

Counting by 5s

Use the number lines to skip count by 5s. Write the correct number in each box.

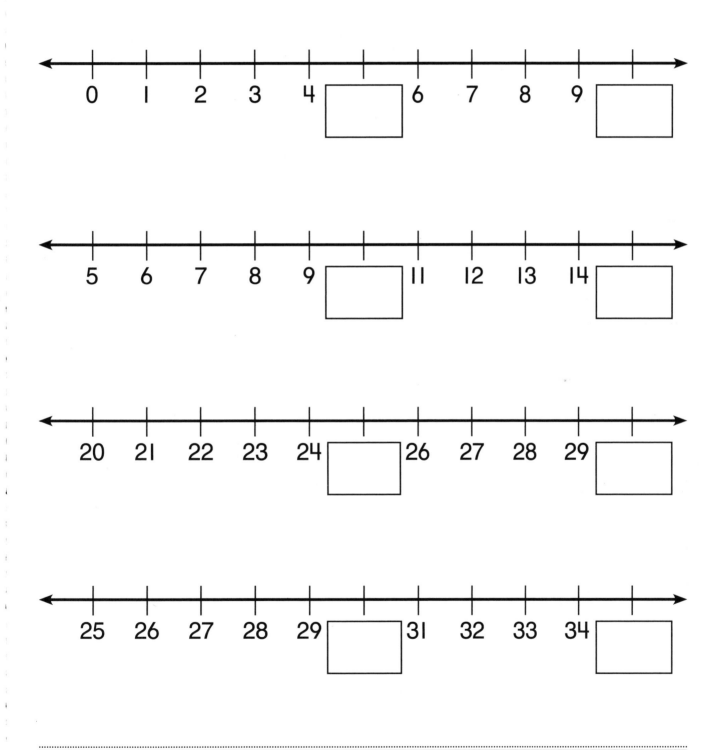

Counting by 5s

Write the missing numbers. Skip count by 5s.

1	2	3	4		6	7	8	9	
11	12	13	14		16	17	18	19	
21	22	23	24		26	27	28	29	
31	32	33	34		36	37	38	39	
41	42	43	44		46	47	48	49	
51	52	53	54		56	57	58	59	
61	62	63	64		66	67	68	69	
71	72	73	74		76	77	78	79	
81	82	83	84		86	87	88	89	
91	92	93	94		96	97	98	99	

CD-104317 • © Carson-Dellosa

Counting by 5s

Complete the pattern. Skip count by 5s.

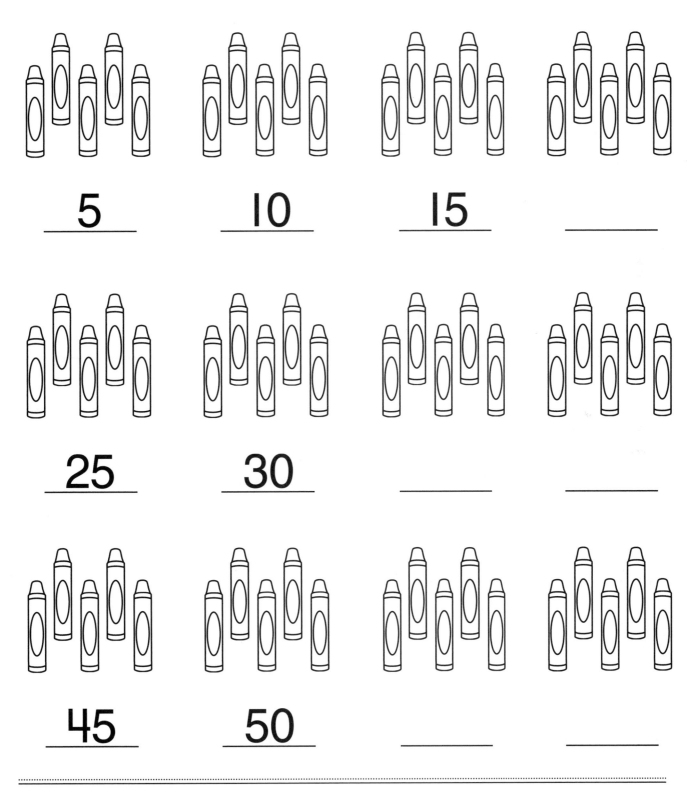

5   10   15   _____

25   30   _____   _____

45   50   _____   _____

Name _____ Date _____

Counting by 5s

Write the missing numbers. Skip count by 5s.

5	10		20
		35	40
	50		
65		75	
	90	95	

Counting by 10s

Use the number lines to skip count by 10s. Write the correct number in each box.

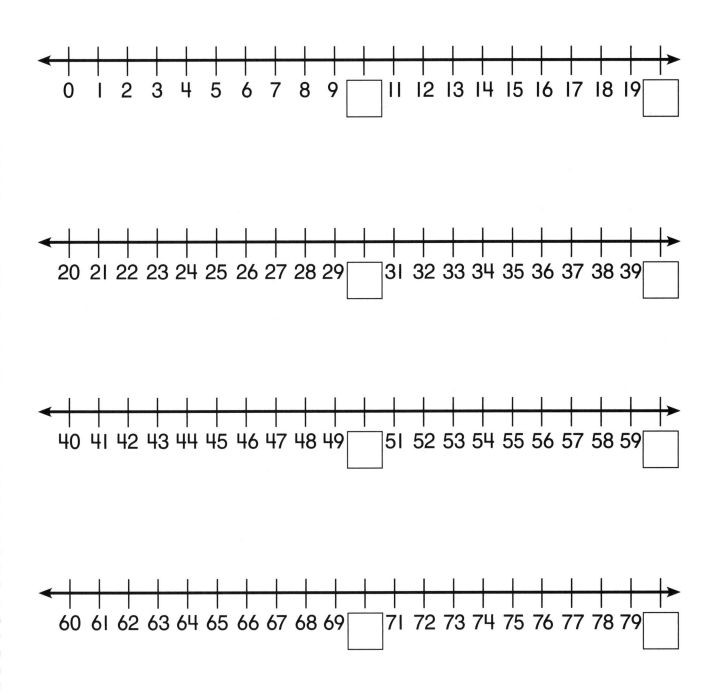

Counting by 10s

Write the missing numbers. Skip count by 10s.

1	2	3	4	5	6	7	8	9	
11	12	13	14	15	16	17	18	19	
21	22	23	24	25	26	27	28	29	
31	32	33	34	35	36	37	38	39	
41	42	43	44	45	46	47	48	49	
51	52	53	54	55	56	57	58	59	
61	62	63	64	65	66	67	68	69	
71	72	73	74	75	76	77	78	79	
81	82	83	84	85	86	87	88	89	
91	92	93	94	95	96	97	98	99	

Counting by 10s

• •

Complete the pattern. Skip count by 10s.

__10__   _____   __30__   _____

__50__   __60__   __70__   _____

_____   __100__   _____   __120__

Counting by 10s

Write the missing numbers. Skip count by 10s.

10			40	50
60		80		100

	20	30		50
60		80	90	

Sums to 6

Total Problems:	**15**
Problems Correct:	_____

Solve each problem.

1. 1
   + 5

2. 2
   + 0

3. 3
   + 1

4. 3
   + 3

5. 3
   + 2

6. 1
   + 2

7. 6
   + 0

8. 2
   + 2

9. 4
   + 0

10. 2
    + 3

11. 1
    + 1

12. 2
    + 4

13. 1
    + 0

14. 2
    + 1

15. 1
    + 3

Name _____   Date _____

Sums to 6

Solve each problem.

1. $2 + 3 =$

2. $1 + 5 =$

3. $4 + 2 =$

4. $0 + 4 =$

5. $1 + 2 =$

6. $1 + 1 =$

7. $2 + 2 =$

8. $3 + 2 =$

9. $4 + 2 =$

10. $5 + 1 =$

11. $3 + 0 =$

12. $3 + 3 =$

Name _____   Date _____

Sums to 8

| Total Problems: | 15 |
| Problems Correct: | _____ |

Solve each problem.

1. 1
   +4

2. 3
   +4

3. 6
   +1

4. 4
   +3

5. 3
   +5

6. 1
   +5

7. 6
   +2

8. 2
   +0

9. 7
   +0

10. 5
    +3

11. 1
    +3

12. 2
    +6

13. 1
    +7

14. 4
    +4

15. 2
    +4

CD-104317 • © Carson-Dellosa

41

Name _____ Date _____

Sums to 8

Solve each problem.

1. $2 + 4 =$

2. $3 + 4 =$

3. $6 + 2 =$

4. $4 + 4 =$

5. $3 + 4 =$

6. $1 + 3 =$

7. $6 + 1 =$

8. $2 + 6 =$

9. $1 + 6 =$

10. $5 + 0 =$

11. $4 + 3 =$

12. $4 + 4 =$

CD-104317 • © Carson-Dellosa

Sums to 10

Solve each problem.

1. $\begin{array}{r} 7 \\ +\,2 \\ \hline \end{array}$
2. $\begin{array}{r} 3 \\ +\,7 \\ \hline \end{array}$
3. $\begin{array}{r} 3 \\ +\,4 \\ \hline \end{array}$
4. $\begin{array}{r} 8 \\ +\,0 \\ \hline \end{array}$
5. $\begin{array}{r} 1 \\ +\,9 \\ \hline \end{array}$

6. $\begin{array}{r} 1 \\ +\,7 \\ \hline \end{array}$
7. $\begin{array}{r} 10 \\ +\,0 \\ \hline \end{array}$
8. $\begin{array}{r} 5 \\ +\,2 \\ \hline \end{array}$
9. $\begin{array}{r} 9 \\ +\,0 \\ \hline \end{array}$
10. $\begin{array}{r} 6 \\ +\,0 \\ \hline \end{array}$

11. $\begin{array}{r} 1 \\ +\,8 \\ \hline \end{array}$
12. $\begin{array}{r} 5 \\ +\,4 \\ \hline \end{array}$
13. $\begin{array}{r} 2 \\ +\,6 \\ \hline \end{array}$
14. $\begin{array}{r} 7 \\ +\,3 \\ \hline \end{array}$
15. $\begin{array}{r} 6 \\ +\,3 \\ \hline \end{array}$

Sums to 10

Solve each problem.

1. $5 + 1 =$

2. $4 + 1 =$

3. $3 + 2 =$

4. $6 + 3 =$

5. $4 + 6 =$

6. $8 + 1 =$

7. $4 + 2 =$

8. $3 + 7 =$

9. $1 + 0 =$

10. $7 + 3 =$

11. $9 + 0 =$

12. $5 + 3 =$

Name _____ Date _____

Sums to 11

Solve each problem.

1. $\begin{array}{r} 5 \\ +4 \\ \hline \end{array}$
2. $\begin{array}{r} 3 \\ +5 \\ \hline \end{array}$
3. $\begin{array}{r} 4 \\ +4 \\ \hline \end{array}$
4. $\begin{array}{r} 7 \\ +3 \\ \hline \end{array}$
5. $\begin{array}{r} 6 \\ +5 \\ \hline \end{array}$

6. $\begin{array}{r} 3 \\ +6 \\ \hline \end{array}$
7. $\begin{array}{r} 6 \\ +4 \\ \hline \end{array}$
8. $\begin{array}{r} 2 \\ +9 \\ \hline \end{array}$
9. $\begin{array}{r} 10 \\ +1 \\ \hline \end{array}$
10. $\begin{array}{r} 1 \\ +1 \\ \hline \end{array}$

11. $\begin{array}{r} 2 \\ +6 \\ \hline \end{array}$
12. $\begin{array}{r} 5 \\ +4 \\ \hline \end{array}$
13. $\begin{array}{r} 4 \\ +7 \\ \hline \end{array}$
14. $\begin{array}{r} 8 \\ +3 \\ \hline \end{array}$
15. $\begin{array}{r} 11 \\ +0 \\ \hline \end{array}$

Sums to 11

Solve each problem.

1. $\begin{array}{r} 9 \\ +2 \\ \hline \end{array}$
2. $\begin{array}{r} 3 \\ +6 \\ \hline \end{array}$
3. $\begin{array}{r} 3 \\ +5 \\ \hline \end{array}$
4. $\begin{array}{r} 11 \\ +0 \\ \hline \end{array}$
5. $\begin{array}{r} 1 \\ +9 \\ \hline \end{array}$

6. $\begin{array}{r} 3 \\ +7 \\ \hline \end{array}$
7. $\begin{array}{r} 10 \\ +1 \\ \hline \end{array}$
8. $\begin{array}{r} 4 \\ +7 \\ \hline \end{array}$
9. $\begin{array}{r} 0 \\ +8 \\ \hline \end{array}$
10. $\begin{array}{r} 9 \\ +0 \\ \hline \end{array}$

11. $\begin{array}{r} 2 \\ +8 \\ \hline \end{array}$
12. $\begin{array}{r} 6 \\ +5 \\ \hline \end{array}$
13. $\begin{array}{r} 5 \\ +6 \\ \hline \end{array}$
14. $\begin{array}{r} 6 \\ +4 \\ \hline \end{array}$
15. $\begin{array}{r} 7 \\ +4 \\ \hline \end{array}$

Sums to 12

Total Problems: **15**
Problems Correct: _____

Solve each problem.

1. $\begin{array}{r} 10 \\ +\ 1 \\ \hline \end{array}$ 2. $\begin{array}{r} 4 \\ +7 \\ \hline \end{array}$ 3. $\begin{array}{r} 3 \\ +6 \\ \hline \end{array}$ 4. $\begin{array}{r} 8 \\ +3 \\ \hline \end{array}$ 5. $\begin{array}{r} 7 \\ +5 \\ \hline \end{array}$

6. $\begin{array}{r} 5 \\ +7 \\ \hline \end{array}$ 7. $\begin{array}{r} 10 \\ +\ 2 \\ \hline \end{array}$ 8. $\begin{array}{r} 3 \\ +7 \\ \hline \end{array}$ 9. $\begin{array}{r} 4 \\ +8 \\ \hline \end{array}$ 10. $\begin{array}{r} 9 \\ +2 \\ \hline \end{array}$

11. $\begin{array}{r} 1 \\ +9 \\ \hline \end{array}$ 12. $\begin{array}{r} 5 \\ +3 \\ \hline \end{array}$ 13. $\begin{array}{r} 6 \\ +6 \\ \hline \end{array}$ 14. $\begin{array}{r} 7 \\ +3 \\ \hline \end{array}$ 15. $\begin{array}{r} 7 \\ +4 \\ \hline \end{array}$

Sums to 12

Total Problems: **15**
Problems Correct: _____

Solve each problem.

1. $\begin{array}{r} 6 \\ +\ 4 \\ \hline \end{array}$

2. $\begin{array}{r} 3 \\ +\ 6 \\ \hline \end{array}$

3. $\begin{array}{r} 3 \\ +\ 5 \\ \hline \end{array}$

4. $\begin{array}{r} 12 \\ +\ 0 \\ \hline \end{array}$

5. $\begin{array}{r} 1 \\ +\ 8 \\ \hline \end{array}$

6. $\begin{array}{r} 3 \\ +\ 7 \\ \hline \end{array}$

7. $\begin{array}{r} 10 \\ +\ 2 \\ \hline \end{array}$

8. $\begin{array}{r} 1 \\ +\ 2 \\ \hline \end{array}$

9. $\begin{array}{r} 7 \\ +\ 1 \\ \hline \end{array}$

10. $\begin{array}{r} 9 \\ +\ 3 \\ \hline \end{array}$

11. $\begin{array}{r} 8 \\ +\ 4 \\ \hline \end{array}$

12. $\begin{array}{r} 5 \\ +\ 6 \\ \hline \end{array}$

13. $\begin{array}{r} 4 \\ +\ 6 \\ \hline \end{array}$

14. $\begin{array}{r} 7 \\ +\ 5 \\ \hline \end{array}$

15. $\begin{array}{r} 7 \\ +\ 4 \\ \hline \end{array}$

Name _____   Date _____

Sums to 13

Total Problems: 15
Problems Correct: _____

Solve each problem.

1.   5
   + 7
   ———

2.   4
   + 7
   ———

3.   8
   + 3
   ———

4.   8
   + 5
   ———

5.   2
   + 9
   ———

6.   3
   + 6
   ———

7.   10
   + 2
   ———

8.   7
   + 6
   ———

9.   6
   + 6
   ———

10.   9
   + 3
   ———

11.   3
   + 8
   ———

12.   8
   + 5
   ———

13.   5
   + 6
   ———

14.   7
   + 4
   ———

15.   7
   + 6
   ———

Sums to 13

Total Problems: **15**
Problems Correct: _____

Solve each problem.

1. $\begin{array}{r} 5 \\ +5 \\ \hline \end{array}$	2. $\begin{array}{r} 5 \\ +7 \\ \hline \end{array}$	3. $\begin{array}{r} 3 \\ +9 \\ \hline \end{array}$	4. $\begin{array}{r} 9 \\ +2 \\ \hline \end{array}$	5. $\begin{array}{r} 2 \\ +9 \\ \hline \end{array}$
6. $\begin{array}{r} 1 \\ +3 \\ \hline \end{array}$	7. $\begin{array}{r} 7 \\ +3 \\ \hline \end{array}$	8. $\begin{array}{r} 6 \\ +7 \\ \hline \end{array}$	9. $\begin{array}{r} 7 \\ +2 \\ \hline \end{array}$	10. $\begin{array}{r} 9 \\ +4 \\ \hline \end{array}$
11. $\begin{array}{r} 4 \\ +8 \\ \hline \end{array}$	12. $\begin{array}{r} 5 \\ +4 \\ \hline \end{array}$	13. $\begin{array}{r} 2 \\ +5 \\ \hline \end{array}$	14. $\begin{array}{r} 7 \\ +1 \\ \hline \end{array}$	15. $\begin{array}{r} 10 \\ +3 \\ \hline \end{array}$

Sums to 14

Solve each problem.

1. $\begin{array}{r} 7 \\ +\,4 \\ \hline \end{array}$ 2. $\begin{array}{r} 6 \\ +\,7 \\ \hline \end{array}$ 3. $\begin{array}{r} 6 \\ +\,6 \\ \hline \end{array}$ 4. $\begin{array}{r} 8 \\ +\,5 \\ \hline \end{array}$ 5. $\begin{array}{r} 2 \\ +\,9 \\ \hline \end{array}$

6. $\begin{array}{r} 5 \\ +\,7 \\ \hline \end{array}$ 7. $\begin{array}{r} 1 \\ +\,4 \\ \hline \end{array}$ 8. $\begin{array}{r} 7 \\ +\,7 \\ \hline \end{array}$ 9. $\begin{array}{r} 7 \\ +\,6 \\ \hline \end{array}$ 10. $\begin{array}{r} 9 \\ +\,4 \\ \hline \end{array}$

11. $\begin{array}{r} 6 \\ +\,8 \\ \hline \end{array}$ 12. $\begin{array}{r} 6 \\ +\,4 \\ \hline \end{array}$ 13. $\begin{array}{r} 6 \\ +\,6 \\ \hline \end{array}$ 14. $\begin{array}{r} 7 \\ +\,7 \\ \hline \end{array}$ 15. $\begin{array}{r} 5 \\ +\,3 \\ \hline \end{array}$

Sums to 14

Solve each problem.

1. $\begin{array}{r} 6 \\ +8 \\ \hline \end{array}$ 2. $\begin{array}{r} 5 \\ +7 \\ \hline \end{array}$ 3. $\begin{array}{r} 3 \\ +9 \\ \hline \end{array}$ 4. $\begin{array}{r} 8 \\ +3 \\ \hline \end{array}$ 5. $\begin{array}{r} 5 \\ +9 \\ \hline \end{array}$

6. $\begin{array}{r} 3 \\ +7 \\ \hline \end{array}$ 7. $\begin{array}{r} 10 \\ +4 \\ \hline \end{array}$ 8. $\begin{array}{r} 7 \\ +7 \\ \hline \end{array}$ 9. $\begin{array}{r} 7 \\ +5 \\ \hline \end{array}$ 10. $\begin{array}{r} 6 \\ +5 \\ \hline \end{array}$

11. $\begin{array}{r} 3 \\ +8 \\ \hline \end{array}$ 12. $\begin{array}{r} 11 \\ +1 \\ \hline \end{array}$ 13. $\begin{array}{r} 6 \\ +6 \\ \hline \end{array}$ 14. $\begin{array}{r} 7 \\ +7 \\ \hline \end{array}$ 15. $\begin{array}{r} 9 \\ +3 \\ \hline \end{array}$

Name _____ Date _____

Sums to 15

Total Problems: **15**
Problems Correct: _____

Solve each problem.

1.   7
   + 6
   ____

2.   7
   + 8
   ____

3.   4
   + 9
   ____

4.   8
   + 7
   ____

5.   9
   + 4
   ____

6.   1
   + 0
   ____

7. 10
   + 5
   ____

8.   5
   + 5
   ____

9.   2
   + 8
   ____

10.   9
   + 6
   ____

11.   1
   + 8
   ____

12.   5
   + 6
   ____

13.   3
   + 6
   ____

14.   3
   + 3
   ____

15.   7
   + 8
   ____

Name _____ Date _____

Sums to 15

Solve each problem.

1. $\begin{array}{r} 5 \\ +7 \\ \hline \end{array}$ 2. $\begin{array}{r} 8 \\ +7 \\ \hline \end{array}$ 3. $\begin{array}{r} 6 \\ +4 \\ \hline \end{array}$ 4. $\begin{array}{r} 6 \\ +9 \\ \hline \end{array}$ 5. $\begin{array}{r} 6 \\ +5 \\ \hline \end{array}$

6. $\begin{array}{r} 3 \\ +7 \\ \hline \end{array}$ 7. $\begin{array}{r} 10 \\ +1 \\ \hline \end{array}$ 8. $\begin{array}{r} 7 \\ +7 \\ \hline \end{array}$ 9. $\begin{array}{r} 7 \\ +2 \\ \hline \end{array}$ 10. $\begin{array}{r} 9 \\ +3 \\ \hline \end{array}$

11. $\begin{array}{r} 12 \\ +3 \\ \hline \end{array}$ 12. $\begin{array}{r} 9 \\ +5 \\ \hline \end{array}$ 13. $\begin{array}{r} 1 \\ +5 \\ \hline \end{array}$ 14. $\begin{array}{r} 7 \\ +4 \\ \hline \end{array}$ 15. $\begin{array}{r} 2 \\ +9 \\ \hline \end{array}$

  CD-104317 • © Carson-Dellosa

Sums to 16

Solve each problem.

1. $\begin{array}{r} 5 \\ +\,9 \\ \hline \end{array}$ 2. $\begin{array}{r} 10 \\ +\,5 \\ \hline \end{array}$ 3. $\begin{array}{r} 8 \\ +\,5 \\ \hline \end{array}$ 4. $\begin{array}{r} 8 \\ +\,7 \\ \hline \end{array}$ 5. $\begin{array}{r} 6 \\ +\,9 \\ \hline \end{array}$

6. $\begin{array}{r} 7 \\ +\,7 \\ \hline \end{array}$ 7. $\begin{array}{r} 10 \\ +\,6 \\ \hline \end{array}$ 8. $\begin{array}{r} 6 \\ +\,4 \\ \hline \end{array}$ 9. $\begin{array}{r} 7 \\ +\,6 \\ \hline \end{array}$ 10. $\begin{array}{r} 10 \\ +\,2 \\ \hline \end{array}$

11. $\begin{array}{r} 8 \\ +\,8 \\ \hline \end{array}$ 12. $\begin{array}{r} 1 \\ +\,6 \\ \hline \end{array}$ 13. $\begin{array}{r} 7 \\ +\,9 \\ \hline \end{array}$ 14. $\begin{array}{r} 9 \\ +\,6 \\ \hline \end{array}$ 15. $\begin{array}{r} 13 \\ +\,3 \\ \hline \end{array}$

Name _____   Date _____

Sums to 16

Solve each problem.

1. $\begin{array}{r} 11 \\ + 5 \\ \hline \end{array}$

2. $\begin{array}{r} 8 \\ + 7 \\ \hline \end{array}$

3. $\begin{array}{r} 7 \\ + 9 \\ \hline \end{array}$

4. $\begin{array}{r} 12 \\ + 4 \\ \hline \end{array}$

5. $\begin{array}{r} 5 \\ + 5 \\ \hline \end{array}$

6. $\begin{array}{r} 6 \\ + 8 \\ \hline \end{array}$

7. $\begin{array}{r} 11 \\ + 2 \\ \hline \end{array}$

8. $\begin{array}{r} 13 \\ + 2 \\ \hline \end{array}$

9. $\begin{array}{r} 4 \\ + 2 \\ \hline \end{array}$

10. $\begin{array}{r} 10 \\ + 6 \\ \hline \end{array}$

11. $\begin{array}{r} 6 \\ + 7 \\ \hline \end{array}$

12. $\begin{array}{r} 5 \\ + 6 \\ \hline \end{array}$

13. $\begin{array}{r} 9 \\ + 5 \\ \hline \end{array}$

14. $\begin{array}{r} 2 \\ + 8 \\ \hline \end{array}$

15. $\begin{array}{r} 9 \\ + 3 \\ \hline \end{array}$

Sums to 17

Solve each problem.

1. 15
   + 1

2. 4
   + 7

3. 9
   + 4

4. 10
   + 7

5. 5
   + 8

6. 4
   + 6

7. 14
   + 3

8. 8
   + 9

9. 3
   + 8

10. 11
    + 4

11. 13
    + 3

12. 5
    + 9

13. 9
    + 8

14. 4
    + 4

15. 15
    + 2

Name _____   Date _____

Sums to 17

Solve each problem.

1. $\begin{array}{r} 7 \\ +\ 6 \\ \hline \end{array}$

2. $\begin{array}{r} 10 \\ +\ 3 \\ \hline \end{array}$

3. $\begin{array}{r} 7 \\ +\ 7 \\ \hline \end{array}$

4. $\begin{array}{r} 13 \\ +\ 4 \\ \hline \end{array}$

5. $\begin{array}{r} 15 \\ +\ 1 \\ \hline \end{array}$

6. $\begin{array}{r} 8 \\ +\ 7 \\ \hline \end{array}$

7. $\begin{array}{r} 11 \\ +\ 4 \\ \hline \end{array}$

8. $\begin{array}{r} 9 \\ +\ 5 \\ \hline \end{array}$

9. $\begin{array}{r} 11 \\ +\ 6 \\ \hline \end{array}$

10. $\begin{array}{r} 12 \\ +\ 5 \\ \hline \end{array}$

11. $\begin{array}{r} 10 \\ +\ 7 \\ \hline \end{array}$

12. $\begin{array}{r} 1 \\ +\ 7 \\ \hline \end{array}$

13. $\begin{array}{r} 7 \\ +\ 9 \\ \hline \end{array}$

14. $\begin{array}{r} 10 \\ +\ 0 \\ \hline \end{array}$

15. $\begin{array}{r} 9 \\ +\ 4 \\ \hline \end{array}$

Name _____ Date _____

Sums to 18

Solve each problem.

1. $\begin{array}{r} 13 \\ + 4 \\ \hline \end{array}$
    2. $\begin{array}{r} 8 \\ + 7 \\ \hline \end{array}$
    3. $\begin{array}{r} 4 \\ + 9 \\ \hline \end{array}$
    4. $\begin{array}{r} 6 \\ + 9 \\ \hline \end{array}$
    5. $\begin{array}{r} 11 \\ + 5 \\ \hline \end{array}$

15

6. $\begin{array}{r} 12 \\ + 1 \\ \hline \end{array}$
    7. $\begin{array}{r} 10 \\ + 8 \\ \hline \end{array}$
    8. $\begin{array}{r} 9 \\ + 5 \\ \hline \end{array}$
    9. $\begin{array}{r} 4 \\ + 7 \\ \hline \end{array}$
    10. $\begin{array}{r} 10 \\ + 2 \\ \hline \end{array}$

11. $\begin{array}{r} 10 \\ + 4 \\ \hline \end{array}$
    12. $\begin{array}{r} 14 \\ + 4 \\ \hline \end{array}$
    13. $\begin{array}{r} 12 \\ + 5 \\ \hline \end{array}$
    14. $\begin{array}{r} 15 \\ + 2 \\ \hline \end{array}$
    15. $\begin{array}{r} 9 \\ + 2 \\ \hline \end{array}$

Sums to 18

Solve each problem.

1.   1
   $\underline{+\ 8}$

2.   15
   $\underline{+\ 3}$

3.   10
   $\underline{+\ 8}$

4.   12
   $\underline{+\ 4}$

5.   8
   $\underline{+\ 9}$

6.   9
   $\underline{+\ 3}$

7.   11
   $\underline{+\ 2}$

8.   11
   $\underline{+\ 7}$

9.   12
   $\underline{+\ 5}$

10.   8
   $\underline{+\ 2}$

11.   8
   $\underline{+\ 5}$

12.   9
   $\underline{+\ 9}$

13.   7
   $\underline{+\ 6}$

14.   9
   $\underline{+\ 7}$

15.   13
   $\underline{+\ 5}$

Name _____ Date _____

Differences from 6 or Less

Solve each problem.

1. $\begin{array}{r} 2 \\ -\,0 \\ \hline \end{array}$ 2. $\begin{array}{r} 5 \\ -\,5 \\ \hline \end{array}$ 3. $\begin{array}{r} 3 \\ -\,1 \\ \hline \end{array}$ 4. $\begin{array}{r} 3 \\ -\,3 \\ \hline \end{array}$ 5. $\begin{array}{r} 3 \\ -\,2 \\ \hline \end{array}$

6. $\begin{array}{r} 5 \\ -\,3 \\ \hline \end{array}$ 7. $\begin{array}{r} 6 \\ -\,0 \\ \hline \end{array}$ 8. $\begin{array}{r} 2 \\ -\,2 \\ \hline \end{array}$ 9. $\begin{array}{r} 4 \\ -\,0 \\ \hline \end{array}$ 10. $\begin{array}{r} 6 \\ -\,3 \\ \hline \end{array}$

11. $\begin{array}{r} 1 \\ -\,1 \\ \hline \end{array}$ 12. $\begin{array}{r} 5 \\ -\,4 \\ \hline \end{array}$ 13. $\begin{array}{r} 1 \\ -\,0 \\ \hline \end{array}$ 14. $\begin{array}{r} 4 \\ -\,1 \\ \hline \end{array}$ 15. $\begin{array}{r} 3 \\ -\,3 \\ \hline \end{array}$

Differences from 6 or Less

Total Problems:	15
Problems Correct:	_____

Solve each problem.

1. $\begin{array}{r} 6 \\ -3 \\ \hline \end{array}$
2. $\begin{array}{r} 2 \\ -2 \\ \hline \end{array}$
3. $\begin{array}{r} 1 \\ -1 \\ \hline \end{array}$
4. $\begin{array}{r} 4 \\ -0 \\ \hline \end{array}$
5. $\begin{array}{r} 4 \\ -2 \\ \hline \end{array}$

6. $\begin{array}{r} 3 \\ -0 \\ \hline \end{array}$
7. $\begin{array}{r} 0 \\ -0 \\ \hline \end{array}$
8. $\begin{array}{r} 5 \\ -4 \\ \hline \end{array}$
9. $\begin{array}{r} 4 \\ -1 \\ \hline \end{array}$
10. $\begin{array}{r} 5 \\ -2 \\ \hline \end{array}$

11. $\begin{array}{r} 6 \\ -4 \\ \hline \end{array}$
12. $\begin{array}{r} 3 \\ -1 \\ \hline \end{array}$
13. $\begin{array}{r} 6 \\ -2 \\ \hline \end{array}$
14. $\begin{array}{r} 4 \\ -3 \\ \hline \end{array}$
15. $\begin{array}{r} 5 \\ -1 \\ \hline \end{array}$

Differences from 10 or Less

Solve each problem.

1. $\begin{array}{r} 8 \\ -5 \\ \hline \end{array}$

2. $\begin{array}{r} 9 \\ -4 \\ \hline \end{array}$

3. $\begin{array}{r} 8 \\ -6 \\ \hline \end{array}$

4. $\begin{array}{r} 10 \\ -3 \\ \hline \end{array}$

5. $\begin{array}{r} 6 \\ -2 \\ \hline \end{array}$

6. $\begin{array}{r} 9 \\ -3 \\ \hline \end{array}$

7. $\begin{array}{r} 7 \\ -5 \\ \hline \end{array}$

8. $\begin{array}{r} 6 \\ -4 \\ \hline \end{array}$

9. $\begin{array}{r} 10 \\ -8 \\ \hline \end{array}$

10. $\begin{array}{r} 4 \\ -2 \\ \hline \end{array}$

11. $\begin{array}{r} 9 \\ -5 \\ \hline \end{array}$

12. $\begin{array}{r} 7 \\ -6 \\ \hline \end{array}$

13. $\begin{array}{r} 8 \\ -4 \\ \hline \end{array}$

14. $\begin{array}{r} 10 \\ -3 \\ \hline \end{array}$

15. $\begin{array}{r} 8 \\ -2 \\ \hline \end{array}$

Differences from 10 or Less

Solve each problem.

1. $\begin{array}{r} 7 \\ -3 \\ \hline \end{array}$
2. $\begin{array}{r} 9 \\ -1 \\ \hline \end{array}$
3. $\begin{array}{r} 10 \\ -4 \\ \hline \end{array}$
4. $\begin{array}{r} 8 \\ -5 \\ \hline \end{array}$
5. $\begin{array}{r} 5 \\ -2 \\ \hline \end{array}$

6. $\begin{array}{r} 9 \\ -8 \\ \hline \end{array}$
7. $\begin{array}{r} 10 \\ -3 \\ \hline \end{array}$
8. $\begin{array}{r} 9 \\ -7 \\ \hline \end{array}$
9. $\begin{array}{r} 9 \\ -5 \\ \hline \end{array}$
10. $\begin{array}{r} 10 \\ -5 \\ \hline \end{array}$

11. $\begin{array}{r} 3 \\ -2 \\ \hline \end{array}$
12. $\begin{array}{r} 10 \\ -10 \\ \hline \end{array}$
13. $\begin{array}{r} 6 \\ -4 \\ \hline \end{array}$
14. $\begin{array}{r} 8 \\ -2 \\ \hline \end{array}$
15. $\begin{array}{r} 9 \\ -2 \\ \hline \end{array}$

Name _____   Date _____

Differences from 11 or Less

Solve each problem.

1. 10
    − 6

2.   9
    − 4

3.   8
    − 8

4.   9
    − 3

5. 11
    − 2

6.   7
    − 3

7.   7
    − 5

8. 11
    − 0

9. 11
    − 1

10. 9
    − 8

11. 9
    − 5

12. 11
    − 2

13. 8
    − 4

14. 11
    − 3

15. 11
    − 6

Differences from 11 or Less

Total Problems: **15**
Problems Correct: _____

Solve each problem.

1. $\begin{array}{r} 10 \\ -\ 4 \\ \hline \end{array}$
2. $\begin{array}{r} 10 \\ -\ 8 \\ \hline \end{array}$
3. $\begin{array}{r} 9 \\ -\ 9 \\ \hline \end{array}$
4. $\begin{array}{r} 11 \\ -\ 3 \\ \hline \end{array}$
5. $\begin{array}{r} 6 \\ -\ 3 \\ \hline \end{array}$

6. $\begin{array}{r} 11 \\ -\ 6 \\ \hline \end{array}$
7. $\begin{array}{r} 11 \\ -\ 11 \\ \hline \end{array}$
8. $\begin{array}{r} 10 \\ -\ 6 \\ \hline \end{array}$
9. $\begin{array}{r} 8 \\ -\ 4 \\ \hline \end{array}$
10. $\begin{array}{r} 11 \\ -\ 8 \\ \hline \end{array}$

11. $\begin{array}{r} 8 \\ -\ 3 \\ \hline \end{array}$
12. $\begin{array}{r} 6 \\ -\ 2 \\ \hline \end{array}$
13. $\begin{array}{r} 10 \\ -\ 4 \\ \hline \end{array}$
14. $\begin{array}{r} 11 \\ -\ 5 \\ \hline \end{array}$
15. $\begin{array}{r} 9 \\ -\ 1 \\ \hline \end{array}$

CD-104317 • © Carson-Dellosa

Name _____ Date _____

Differences from 12 or Less

Total Problems: **15**
Problems Correct: _____

Solve each problem.

1. $\begin{array}{r} 12 \\ -\ 8 \\ \hline \end{array}$
2. $\begin{array}{r} 9 \\ -2 \\ \hline \end{array}$
3. $\begin{array}{r} 10 \\ -\ 9 \\ \hline \end{array}$
4. $\begin{array}{r} 11 \\ -\ 5 \\ \hline \end{array}$
5. $\begin{array}{r} 9 \\ -5 \\ \hline \end{array}$

6. $\begin{array}{r} 9 \\ -4 \\ \hline \end{array}$
7. $\begin{array}{r} 10 \\ -\ 5 \\ \hline \end{array}$
8. $\begin{array}{r} 11 \\ -\ 4 \\ \hline \end{array}$
9. $\begin{array}{r} 11 \\ -\ 1 \\ \hline \end{array}$
10. $\begin{array}{r} 12 \\ -\ 3 \\ \hline \end{array}$

11. $\begin{array}{r} 10 \\ -\ 4 \\ \hline \end{array}$
12. $\begin{array}{r} 8 \\ -3 \\ \hline \end{array}$
13. $\begin{array}{r} 12 \\ -\ 4 \\ \hline \end{array}$
14. $\begin{array}{r} 12 \\ -\ 0 \\ \hline \end{array}$
15. $\begin{array}{r} 9 \\ -6 \\ \hline \end{array}$

Differences from 12 or Less

Total Problems:	15
Problems Correct:	_____

Solve each problem.

1. 11
   − 7

2. 9
   − 8

3. 10
   − 5

4. 12
   − 5

5. 12
   − 12

6. 9
   − 6

7. 9
   − 2

8. 11
   − 2

9. 12
   − 3

10. 8
    − 6

11. 12
    − 2

12. 7
    − 4

13. 9
    − 5

14. 7
    − 2

15. 9
    − 3

CD-104317 • © Carson-Dellosa

Differences from 13 or Less

Solve each problem.

1. $\begin{array}{r} 13 \\ -\ 6 \\ \hline \end{array}$ 2. $\begin{array}{r} 12 \\ -\ 4 \\ \hline \end{array}$ 3. $\begin{array}{r} 12 \\ -\ 6 \\ \hline \end{array}$ 4. $\begin{array}{r} 13 \\ -\ 3 \\ \hline \end{array}$ 5. $\begin{array}{r} 10 \\ -\ 3 \\ \hline \end{array}$

6. $\begin{array}{r} 8 \\ -3 \\ \hline \end{array}$ 7. $\begin{array}{r} 9 \\ -3 \\ \hline \end{array}$ 8. $\begin{array}{r} 9 \\ -4 \\ \hline \end{array}$ 9. $\begin{array}{r} 13 \\ -\ 5 \\ \hline \end{array}$ 10. $\begin{array}{r} 10 \\ -\ 5 \\ \hline \end{array}$

11. $\begin{array}{r} 8 \\ -5 \\ \hline \end{array}$ 12. $\begin{array}{r} 10 \\ -\ 6 \\ \hline \end{array}$ 13. $\begin{array}{r} 8 \\ -1 \\ \hline \end{array}$ 14. $\begin{array}{r} 11 \\ -\ 3 \\ \hline \end{array}$ 15. $\begin{array}{r} 9 \\ -5 \\ \hline \end{array}$

Name _____   Date _____

Differences from 13 or Less

Total Problems: 15
Problems Correct: _____

Solve each problem.

1. 9
   − 7

2. 9
   − 6

3. 10
   − 4

4. 9
   − 3

5. 13
   − 5

6. 13
   − 6

7. 10
   − 3

8. 13
   − 7

9. 9
   − 4

10. 0
    − 0

11. 7
    − 3

12. 8
    − 2

13. 9
    − 4

14. 9
    − 2

15. 3
    − 2

        CD-104317 • © Carson-Dellosa

Name _____ Date _____

Differences from 14 or Less

Total Problems: 15
Problems Correct: _____

Solve each problem.

1. $\begin{array}{r} 12 \\ -\ 8 \\ \hline \end{array}$	2. $\begin{array}{r} 12 \\ -\ 5 \\ \hline \end{array}$	3. $\begin{array}{r} 12 \\ -\ 3 \\ \hline \end{array}$	4. $\begin{array}{r} 9 \\ -\ 2 \\ \hline \end{array}$	5. $\begin{array}{r} 13 \\ -\ 1 \\ \hline \end{array}$
6. $\begin{array}{r} 10 \\ -\ 2 \\ \hline \end{array}$	7. $\begin{array}{r} 14 \\ -\ 7 \\ \hline \end{array}$	8. $\begin{array}{r} 14 \\ -\ 14 \\ \hline \end{array}$	9. $\begin{array}{r} 10 \\ -\ 5 \\ \hline \end{array}$	10. $\begin{array}{r} 14 \\ -\ 3 \\ \hline \end{array}$
11. $\begin{array}{r} 10 \\ -\ 7 \\ \hline \end{array}$	12. $\begin{array}{r} 14 \\ -\ 5 \\ \hline \end{array}$	13. $\begin{array}{r} 11 \\ -\ 6 \\ \hline \end{array}$	14. $\begin{array}{r} 11 \\ -\ 9 \\ \hline \end{array}$	15. $\begin{array}{r} 14 \\ -\ 6 \\ \hline \end{array}$

Name _____ Date _____

Differences from 14 or Less

Solve each problem.

1. 10
   − 4
   ___

2. 13
   − 8
   ___

3. 14
   − 2
   ___

4. 11
   − 8
   ___

5. 10
   − 6
   ___

6. 13
   − 5
   ___

7. 9
   − 3
   ___

8. 11
   − 5
   ___

9. 9
   − 5
   ___

10. 14
   − 6
   ___

11. 12
   − 9
   ___

12. 11
   − 7
   ___

13. 14
   − 7
   ___

14. 10
   − 8
   ___

15. 12
   − 4
   ___

Differences from 15 or Less

Total Problems:	15
Problems Correct:	_____

Solve each problem.

1. $\begin{array}{r} 14 \\ -\ 4 \\ \hline \end{array}$
2. $\begin{array}{r} 12 \\ -\ 4 \\ \hline \end{array}$
3. $\begin{array}{r} 15 \\ -\ 3 \\ \hline \end{array}$
4. $\begin{array}{r} 14 \\ -\ 6 \\ \hline \end{array}$
5. $\begin{array}{r} 10 \\ -\ 3 \\ \hline \end{array}$

6. $\begin{array}{r} 15 \\ -\ 8 \\ \hline \end{array}$
7. $\begin{array}{r} 15 \\ -\ 5 \\ \hline \end{array}$
8. $\begin{array}{r} 13 \\ -\ 3 \\ \hline \end{array}$
9. $\begin{array}{r} 10 \\ -\ 5 \\ \hline \end{array}$
10. $\begin{array}{r} 11 \\ -\ 5 \\ \hline \end{array}$

11. $\begin{array}{r} 15 \\ -\ 2 \\ \hline \end{array}$
12. $\begin{array}{r} 11 \\ -\ 6 \\ \hline \end{array}$
13. $\begin{array}{r} 10 \\ -\ 1 \\ \hline \end{array}$
14. $\begin{array}{r} 11 \\ -\ 3 \\ \hline \end{array}$
15. $\begin{array}{r} 12 \\ -\ 6 \\ \hline \end{array}$

Differences from 15 or Less

Solve each problem.

1. $15 - 2$

2. $15 - 6$

3. $13 - 4$

4. $15 - 3$

5. $10 - 3$

6. $14 - 6$

7. $12 - 8$

8. $13 - 5$

9. $15 - 15$

10. $10 - 8$

11. $12 - 3$

12. $11 - 2$

13. $11 - 5$

14. $13 - 6$

15. $10 - 2$

  CD-104317 • © Carson-Dellosa

Differences from 16 or Less

Solve each problem.

1. 13
    $-\ 2$

2. 13
    $-\ 8$

3. 15
    $-\ 9$

4. 12
    $-\ 8$

5. 10
    $-\ 6$

6. 16
    $-\ 9$

7. 10
    $-\ 7$

8. 13
    $-\ 3$

9. 11
    $-\ 5$

10. 11
    $-\ 9$

11. 10
    $-\ 8$

12. 12
    $-\ 3$

13. 16
    $-\ 5$

14. 16
    $-\ 4$

15. 12
    $-\ 2$

Differences from 16 or Less

Solve each problem.

1. 14
    $-\ 4$

2. 15
    $-\ 2$

3. 14
    $-\ 4$

4. 16
    $-\ 16$

5. 15
    $-\ 3$

6. 12
    $-\ 6$

7. 15
    $-\ 3$

8. 14
    $-\ 7$

9. 16
    $-\ 4$

10. 12
    $-\ 8$

11. 16
    $-\ 3$

12. 13
    $-\ 2$

13. 16
    $-\ 5$

14. 13
    $-\ 2$

15. 12
    $-\ 6$

Differences from 17 or Less

Solve each problem.

1. 16
  − 1

2. 11
  − 3

3. 11
  − 6

4. 15
  − 3

5. 10
  − 3

6. 17
  − 6

7. 13
  − 8

8. 15
  − 4

9. 16
  − 5

10. 17
   − 5

11. 13
   − 9

12. 15
   − 4

13. 17
   − 6

14. 14
   − 3

15. 14
   − 4

Name _____ Date _____

Differences from 17 or Less

Solve each problem.

1. $\begin{array}{r} 13 \\ -\ 3 \\ \hline \end{array}$

2. $\begin{array}{r} 12 \\ -\ 4 \\ \hline \end{array}$

3. $\begin{array}{r} 17 \\ -\ 5 \\ \hline \end{array}$

4. $\begin{array}{r} 12 \\ -\ 8 \\ \hline \end{array}$

5. $\begin{array}{r} 17 \\ -\ 5 \\ \hline \end{array}$

6. $\begin{array}{r} 15 \\ -\ 5 \\ \hline \end{array}$

7. $\begin{array}{r} 16 \\ -\ 9 \\ \hline \end{array}$

8. $\begin{array}{r} 17 \\ -\ 8 \\ \hline \end{array}$

9. $\begin{array}{r} 13 \\ -\ 7 \\ \hline \end{array}$

10. $\begin{array}{r} 15 \\ -\ 2 \\ \hline \end{array}$

11. $\begin{array}{r} 15 \\ -\ 9 \\ \hline \end{array}$

12. $\begin{array}{r} 17 \\ -\ 7 \\ \hline \end{array}$

13. $\begin{array}{r} 17 \\ -\ 17 \\ \hline \end{array}$

14. $\begin{array}{r} 14 \\ -\ 2 \\ \hline \end{array}$

15. $\begin{array}{r} 11 \\ -\ 8 \\ \hline \end{array}$

Name _____ Date _____

Differences from 18 or Less

Solve each problem.

1. $\begin{array}{r} 10 \\ -\ 6 \\ \hline \end{array}$

2. $\begin{array}{r} 12 \\ -\ 7 \\ \hline \end{array}$

3. $\begin{array}{r} 13 \\ -\ 4 \\ \hline \end{array}$

4. $\begin{array}{r} 14 \\ -\ 4 \\ \hline \end{array}$

5. $\begin{array}{r} 14 \\ -\ 8 \\ \hline \end{array}$

6. $\begin{array}{r} 12 \\ -\ 5 \\ \hline \end{array}$

7. $\begin{array}{r} 16 \\ -\ 5 \\ \hline \end{array}$

8. $\begin{array}{r} 18 \\ -\ 9 \\ \hline \end{array}$

9. $\begin{array}{r} 10 \\ -\ 2 \\ \hline \end{array}$

10. $\begin{array}{r} 17 \\ -\ 3 \\ \hline \end{array}$

11. $\begin{array}{r} 11 \\ -\ 3 \\ \hline \end{array}$

12. $\begin{array}{r} 18 \\ -\ 7 \\ \hline \end{array}$

13. $\begin{array}{r} 15 \\ -\ 7 \\ \hline \end{array}$

14. $\begin{array}{r} 16 \\ -\ 9 \\ \hline \end{array}$

15. $\begin{array}{r} 18 \\ -\ 3 \\ \hline \end{array}$

Differences from 18 or Less

Total Problems:	15
Problems Correct:	_____

Solve each problem.

1. $\begin{array}{r} 14 \\ -\ 2 \\ \hline \end{array}$
2. $\begin{array}{r} 12 \\ -\ 2 \\ \hline \end{array}$
3. $\begin{array}{r} 17 \\ -\ 8 \\ \hline \end{array}$
4. $\begin{array}{r} 18 \\ -\ 18 \\ \hline \end{array}$
5. $\begin{array}{r} 18 \\ -\ 1 \\ \hline \end{array}$

6. $\begin{array}{r} 10 \\ -\ 3 \\ \hline \end{array}$
7. $\begin{array}{r} 17 \\ -\ 4 \\ \hline \end{array}$
8. $\begin{array}{r} 16 \\ -\ 4 \\ \hline \end{array}$
9. $\begin{array}{r} 14 \\ -\ 3 \\ \hline \end{array}$
10. $\begin{array}{r} 18 \\ -\ 2 \\ \hline \end{array}$

11. $\begin{array}{r} 17 \\ -\ 6 \\ \hline \end{array}$
12. $\begin{array}{r} 15 \\ -\ 6 \\ \hline \end{array}$
13. $\begin{array}{r} 18 \\ -\ 2 \\ \hline \end{array}$
14. $\begin{array}{r} 15 \\ -\ 7 \\ \hline \end{array}$
15. $\begin{array}{r} 16 \\ -\ 5 \\ \hline \end{array}$

 CD-104317 • © Carson-Dellosa

Name _____ Date _____

Addition and Subtraction through 10

Solve each problem.

1. $\begin{array}{r} 6 \\ -6 \\ \hline \end{array}$

2. $\begin{array}{r} 8 \\ +2 \\ \hline \end{array}$

3. $\begin{array}{r} 8 \\ -5 \\ \hline \end{array}$

4. $\begin{array}{r} 7 \\ +2 \\ \hline \end{array}$

5. $\begin{array}{r} 7 \\ +3 \\ \hline \end{array}$

6. $\begin{array}{r} 8 \\ +0 \\ \hline \end{array}$

7. $\begin{array}{r} 9 \\ -3 \\ \hline \end{array}$

8. $\begin{array}{r} 10 \\ -6 \\ \hline \end{array}$

9. $\begin{array}{r} 9 \\ +0 \\ \hline \end{array}$

10. $\begin{array}{r} 4 \\ +3 \\ \hline \end{array}$

11. $\begin{array}{r} 10 \\ -6 \\ \hline \end{array}$

12. $\begin{array}{r} 2 \\ +3 \\ \hline \end{array}$

13. $\begin{array}{r} 5 \\ -2 \\ \hline \end{array}$

14. $\begin{array}{r} 9 \\ +1 \\ \hline \end{array}$

15. $\begin{array}{r} 2 \\ -2 \\ \hline \end{array}$

Addition and Subtraction through 10

Total Problems:	15
Problems Correct:	_____

Solve each problem.

1. $\begin{array}{r} 7 \\ +\,2 \\ \hline \end{array}$

2. $\begin{array}{r} 9 \\ +\,1 \\ \hline \end{array}$

3. $\begin{array}{r} 5 \\ -\,3 \\ \hline \end{array}$

4. $\begin{array}{r} 8 \\ +\,1 \\ \hline \end{array}$

5. $\begin{array}{r} 10 \\ +\,0 \\ \hline \end{array}$

6. $\begin{array}{r} 9 \\ -\,3 \\ \hline \end{array}$

7. $\begin{array}{r} 5 \\ -\,2 \\ \hline \end{array}$

8. $\begin{array}{r} 10 \\ -\,2 \\ \hline \end{array}$

9. $\begin{array}{r} 7 \\ +\,0 \\ \hline \end{array}$

10. $\begin{array}{r} 7 \\ +\,1 \\ \hline \end{array}$

11. $\begin{array}{r} 9 \\ -\,6 \\ \hline \end{array}$

12. $\begin{array}{r} 2 \\ +\,2 \\ \hline \end{array}$

13. $\begin{array}{r} 8 \\ -\,3 \\ \hline \end{array}$

14. $\begin{array}{r} 6 \\ +\,2 \\ \hline \end{array}$

15. $\begin{array}{r} 7 \\ -\,5 \\ \hline \end{array}$

 CD-104317 • © Carson-Dellosa

Addition and Subtraction through 10

Total Problems:	15
Problems Correct:	_____

Solve each problem.

1. $\begin{array}{r} 8 \\ +1 \\ \hline \end{array}$

2. $\begin{array}{r} 8 \\ +2 \\ \hline \end{array}$

3. $\begin{array}{r} 5 \\ -2 \\ \hline \end{array}$

4. $\begin{array}{r} 9 \\ -5 \\ \hline \end{array}$

5. $\begin{array}{r} 9 \\ +0 \\ \hline \end{array}$

6. $\begin{array}{r} 6 \\ -2 \\ \hline \end{array}$

7. $\begin{array}{r} 5 \\ -3 \\ \hline \end{array}$

8. $\begin{array}{r} 8 \\ -3 \\ \hline \end{array}$

9. $\begin{array}{r} 7 \\ +1 \\ \hline \end{array}$

10. $\begin{array}{r} 8 \\ +1 \\ \hline \end{array}$

11. $\begin{array}{r} 9 \\ -6 \\ \hline \end{array}$

12. $\begin{array}{r} 4 \\ +2 \\ \hline \end{array}$

13. $\begin{array}{r} 8 \\ -2 \\ \hline \end{array}$

14. $\begin{array}{r} 3 \\ -2 \\ \hline \end{array}$

15. $\begin{array}{r} 9 \\ +1 \\ \hline \end{array}$

One-Digit Addition without Regrouping

Solve each problem.

1.   5
  +4

2.   7
  +0

3.   6
  +1

4.   3
  +1

5.   3
  +6

6.   4
  +4

7.   2
  +7

8.   8
  +1

9.   5
  +3

10.   7
  +1

11.   8
  +0

12.   6
  +2

13.   5
  +2

14.   4
  +3

15.   3
  +5

One-Digit Addition with Regrouping

Total Problems: 15
Problems Correct: _____

Solve each problem.

1. 2
   + 8
   ____

2. 7
   + 8
   ____

3. 6
   + 8
   ____

4. 6
   + 5
   ____

5. 3
   + 9
   ____

6. 4
   + 7
   ____

7. 9
   + 9
   ____

8. 8
   + 5
   ____

9. 9
   + 8
   ____

10. 7
    + 6
    ____

11. 8
    + 8
    ____

12. 6
    + 7
    ____

13. 5
    + 6
    ____

14. 4
    + 7
    ____

15. 8
    + 7
    ____

Two-Digit Addition without Regrouping

Total Problems:	15
Problems Correct:	_____

Solve each problem.

1. $\begin{array}{r} 15 \\ +\ 4 \\ \hline \end{array}$
2. $\begin{array}{r} 12 \\ +\ 7 \\ \hline \end{array}$
3. $\begin{array}{r} 17 \\ +\ 1 \\ \hline \end{array}$
4. $\begin{array}{r} 12 \\ +\ 3 \\ \hline \end{array}$
5. $\begin{array}{r} 10 \\ +\ 5 \\ \hline \end{array}$

6. $\begin{array}{r} 15 \\ +\ 2 \\ \hline \end{array}$
7. $\begin{array}{r} 11 \\ +\ 8 \\ \hline \end{array}$
8. $\begin{array}{r} 11 \\ +\ 6 \\ \hline \end{array}$
9. $\begin{array}{r} 13 \\ +\ 5 \\ \hline \end{array}$
10. $\begin{array}{r} 10 \\ +\ 7 \\ \hline \end{array}$

11. $\begin{array}{r} 10 \\ +\ 2 \\ \hline \end{array}$
12. $\begin{array}{r} 16 \\ +\ 2 \\ \hline \end{array}$
13. $\begin{array}{r} 14 \\ +\ 3 \\ \hline \end{array}$
14. $\begin{array}{r} 12 \\ +\ 1 \\ \hline \end{array}$
15. $\begin{array}{r} 14 \\ +\ 4 \\ \hline \end{array}$

Name _____ Date _____

Two-Digit Addition with Regrouping

Total Problems: **15**

Problems Correct: _____

Solve each problem.

1. $\begin{array}{r} 11 \\ + 9 \\ \hline \end{array}$

2. $\begin{array}{r} 14 \\ + 8 \\ \hline \end{array}$

3. $\begin{array}{r} 15 \\ + 8 \\ \hline \end{array}$

4. $\begin{array}{r} 15 \\ + 6 \\ \hline \end{array}$

5. $\begin{array}{r} 13 \\ + 9 \\ \hline \end{array}$

6. $\begin{array}{r} 17 \\ + 4 \\ \hline \end{array}$

7. $\begin{array}{r} 19 \\ + 7 \\ \hline \end{array}$

8. $\begin{array}{r} 16 \\ + 5 \\ \hline \end{array}$

9. $\begin{array}{r} 14 \\ + 9 \\ \hline \end{array}$

10. $\begin{array}{r} 18 \\ + 6 \\ \hline \end{array}$

11. $\begin{array}{r} 12 \\ + 8 \\ \hline \end{array}$

12. $\begin{array}{r} 17 \\ + 6 \\ \hline \end{array}$

13. $\begin{array}{r} 15 \\ + 7 \\ \hline \end{array}$

14. $\begin{array}{r} 13 \\ + 7 \\ \hline \end{array}$

15. $\begin{array}{r} 16 \\ + 6 \\ \hline \end{array}$

Telling Time to the Hour

Write the correct time under each clock.

__ __ : __ __   __ __ : __ __   __ __ : __ __

__ __ : __ __   __ __ : __ __   __ __ : __ __

Name _____   Date _____

Telling Time to the Hour

Write the correct time under each clock.

___ : ___ ___   ___ : ___ ___   ___ : ___ ___

___ ___ : ___ ___   ___ ___ : ___ ___   ___ : ___ ___

Telling Time to the Half Hour

Write the correct time under each clock.

___ : ___ ___   ___ : ___ ___   ___ ___ : ___ ___

___ : ___ ___   ___ : ___ ___   ___ : ___ ___

   CD-104317 • © Carson-Dellosa

Telling Time to the Half Hour

· ·

Write the correct time under each clock.

__ __ : __ __ __   __ __ : __ __ __   __ __ : __ __ __

__ __ __ : __ __ __   __ __ __ : __ __ __   __ __ : __ __ __

Telling Time to the Hour

Draw hands on each clock to show the correct time.

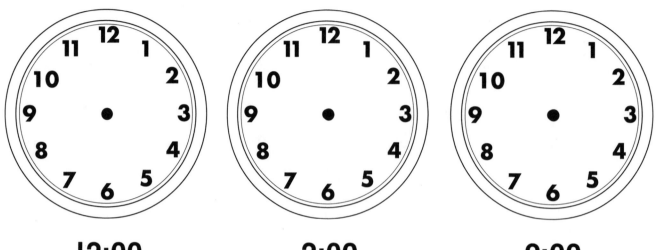

| 12:00 | 2:00 | 9:00 |

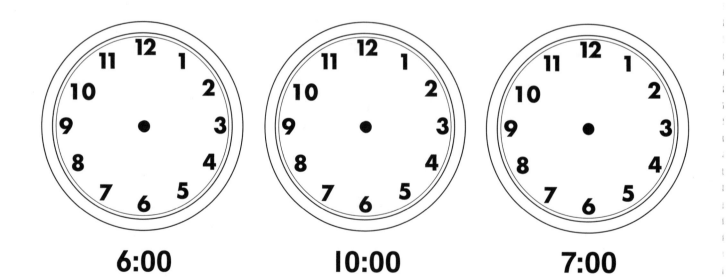

| 6:00 | 10:00 | 7:00 |

CD-104317 • © Carson-Dellosa

Telling Time to the Half Hour

Draw hands on each clock to show the correct time.

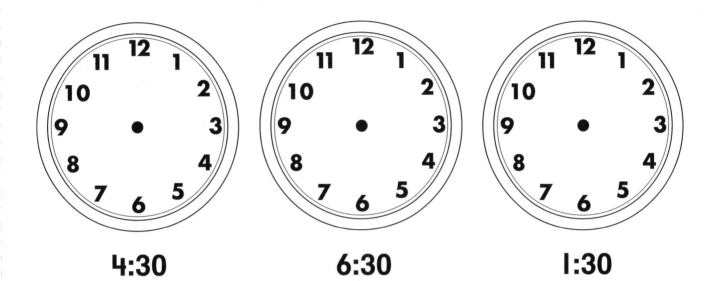

4:30   **6:30**   **1:30**

10:30   **9:30**   **12:30**

Naming Shapes

• •

Draw a line from each shape to its name.

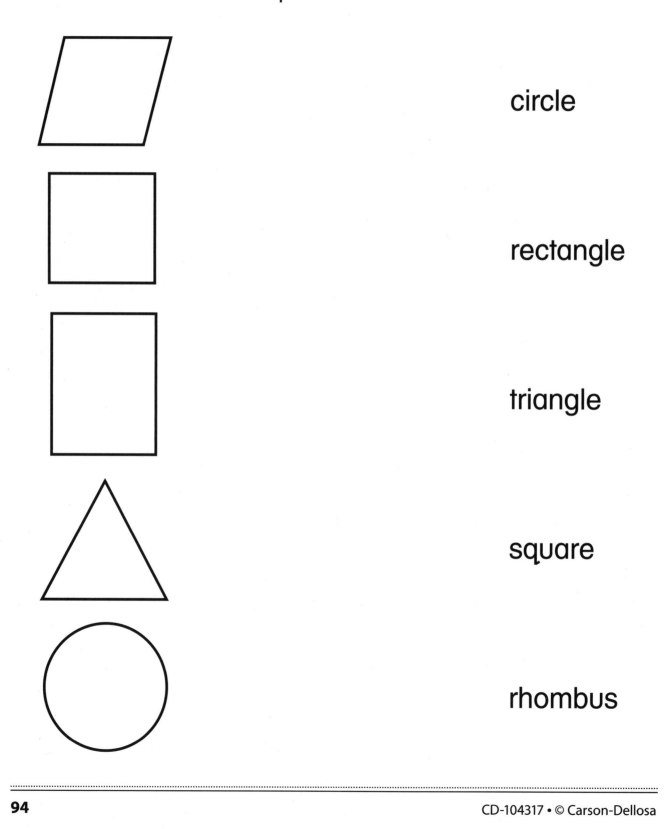

circle

rectangle

triangle

square

rhombus

Name _____ Date _____

Recognizing Shapes

Color all of the circles blue. Color all of the triangles red. Color all of the rectangles green. Color all of the squares orange.

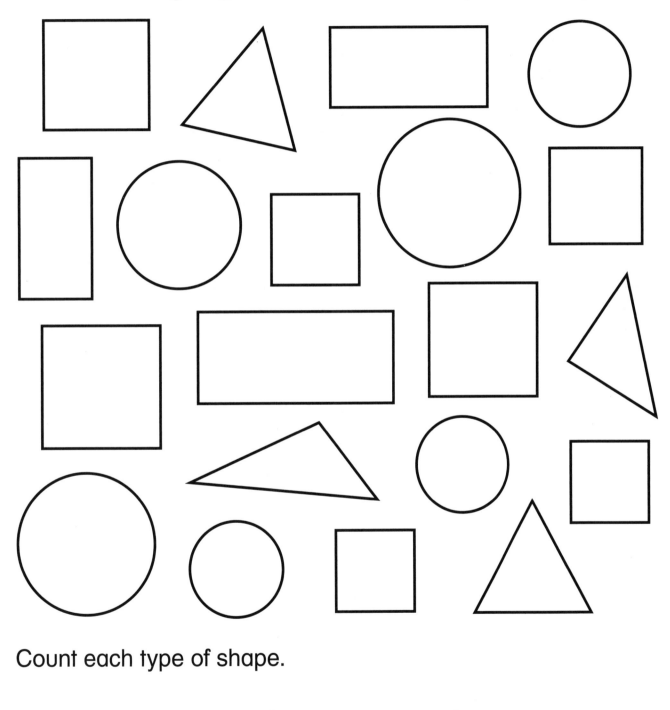

Count each type of shape.

_____ circles   _____ triangles   _____ rectangles   _____ squares

Name _____ Date _____

Extending Patterns

Draw what comes next on the lines.

_____ _____

_____ _____

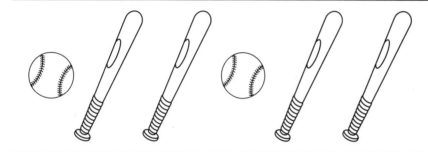

_____ _____

_____ _____

_____ _____

Describing Patterns

Use the letters **A**, **B**, and **C** to describe each pattern.

___ ___ ___ ___ ___ ___ ___ ___

___ ___ ___ ___ ___ ___ ___ ___

___ ___ ___ ___ ___ ___

___ ___ ___ ___ ___ ___ ___ ___ ___

___ ___ ___ ___ ___ ___ ___ ___

Measuring with Units

Write how long each object is in units.

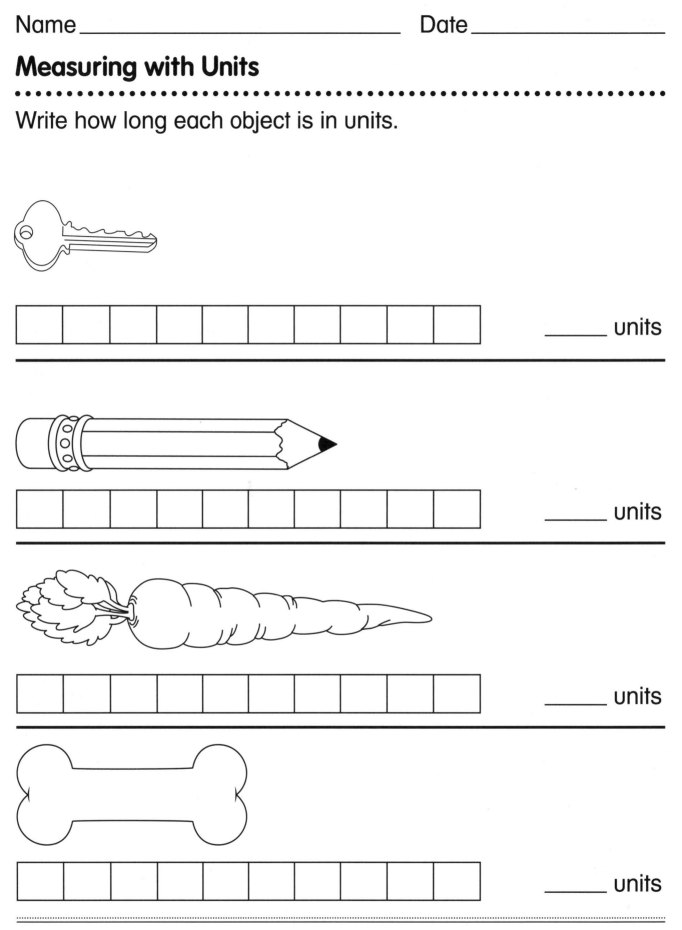

_____ units

_____ units

_____ units

_____ units

Measuring with Inches

Write how long each object is in inches.

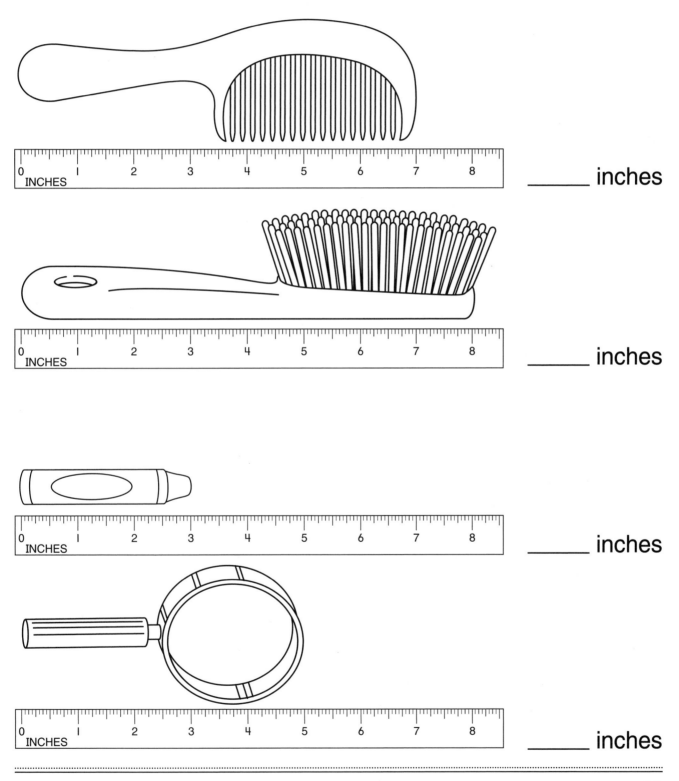

_____ inches

_____ inches

_____ inches

_____ inches

Measuring with Centimeters

Measure each object.
Write how long each object is in centimeters.

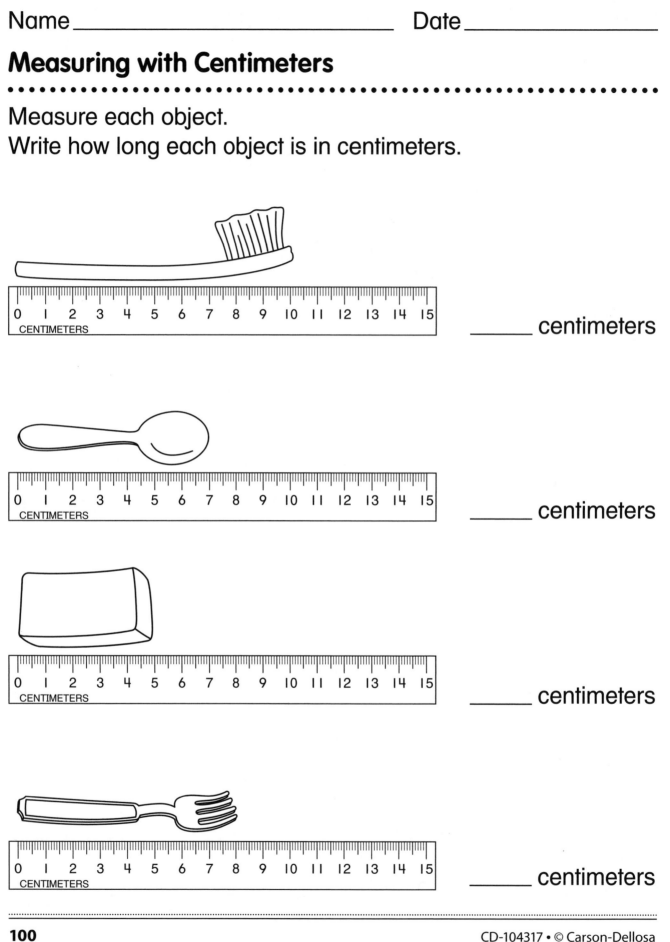

_____ centimeters

_____ centimeters

_____ centimeters

_____ centimeters

Parts of a Whole

Write how much of each shape is shaded.
The total number of parts goes on the bottom of the fraction.
The number of shaded parts goes on the top of the fraction.

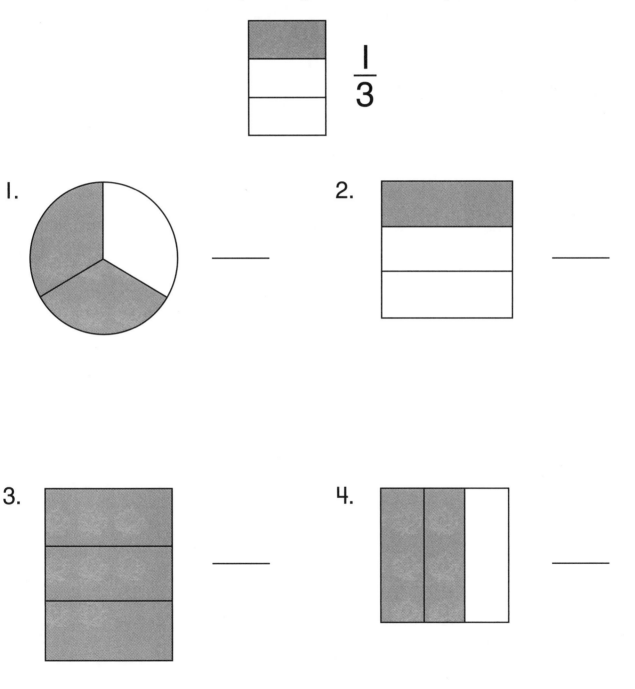

$\dfrac{1}{3}$

1.

2.

3.

4.

Name _____ Date _____

Parts of a Whole

Write how much of each shape is shaded.
The total number of parts goes on the bottom of the fraction.
The number of shaded parts goes on the top of the fraction.

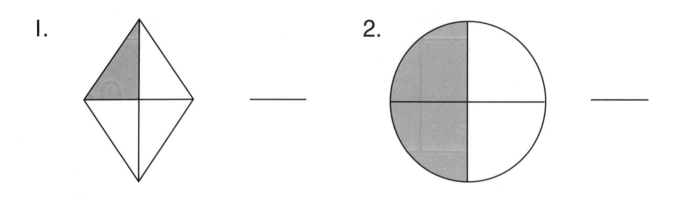

1.   2.

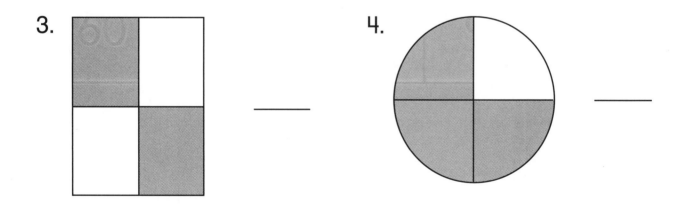

3.   4.

CD-104317 • © Carson-Dellosa

Parts of a Whole

Color each shape to show the fraction.

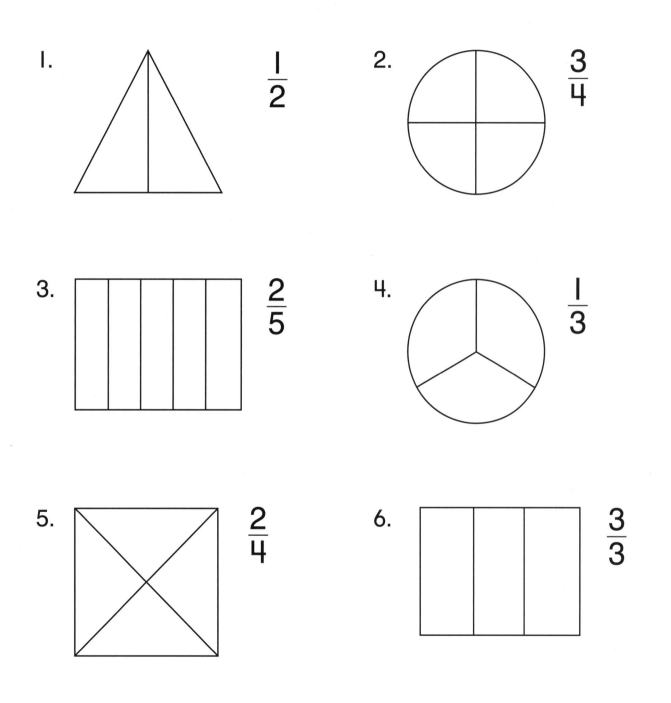

1. $\dfrac{1}{2}$

2. $\dfrac{3}{4}$

3. $\dfrac{2}{5}$

4. $\dfrac{1}{3}$

5. $\dfrac{2}{4}$

6. $\dfrac{3}{3}$

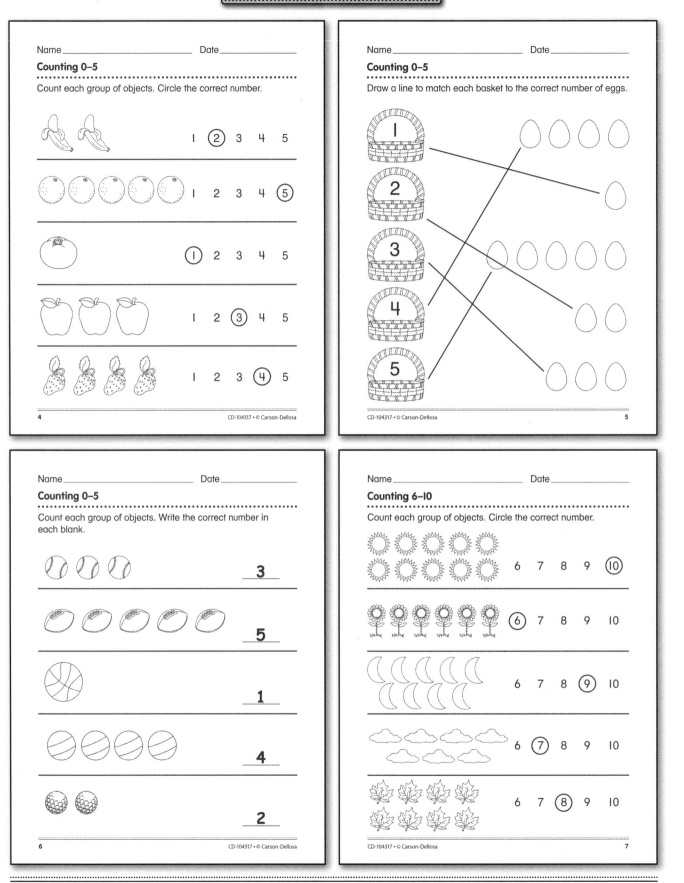

Name_____ Date_____

Counting 0–5

Count each group of objects. Circle the correct number.

1　②　3　4　5

1　2　3　4　⑤

①　2　3　4　5

1　2　③　4　5

1　2　3　④　5

4　　CD-104317 • © Carson-Dellosa

Name_____ Date_____

Counting 0–5

Draw a line to match each basket to the correct number of eggs.

1
2
3
4
5

CD-104317 • © Carson-Dellosa　　5

Name_____ Date_____

Counting 0–5

Count each group of objects. Write the correct number in each blank.

3

5

1

4

2

6　　CD-104317 • © Carson-Dellosa

Name_____ Date_____

Counting 6–10

Count each group of objects. Circle the correct number.

6　7　8　9　⑩

⑥　7　8　9　10

6　7　8　⑨　10

6　⑦　8　9　10

6　7　⑧　9　10

CD-104317 • © Carson-Dellosa　　7

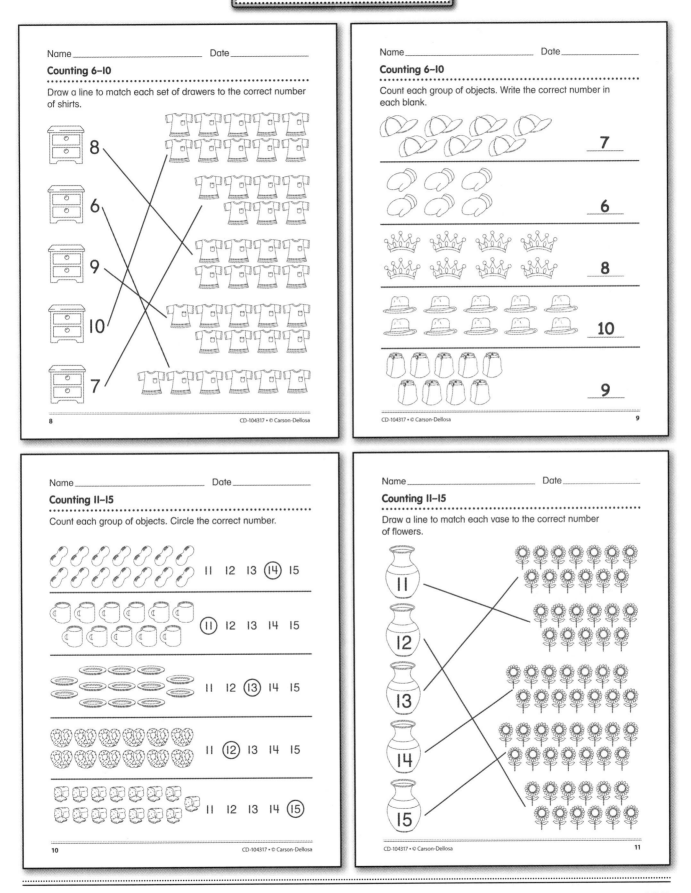

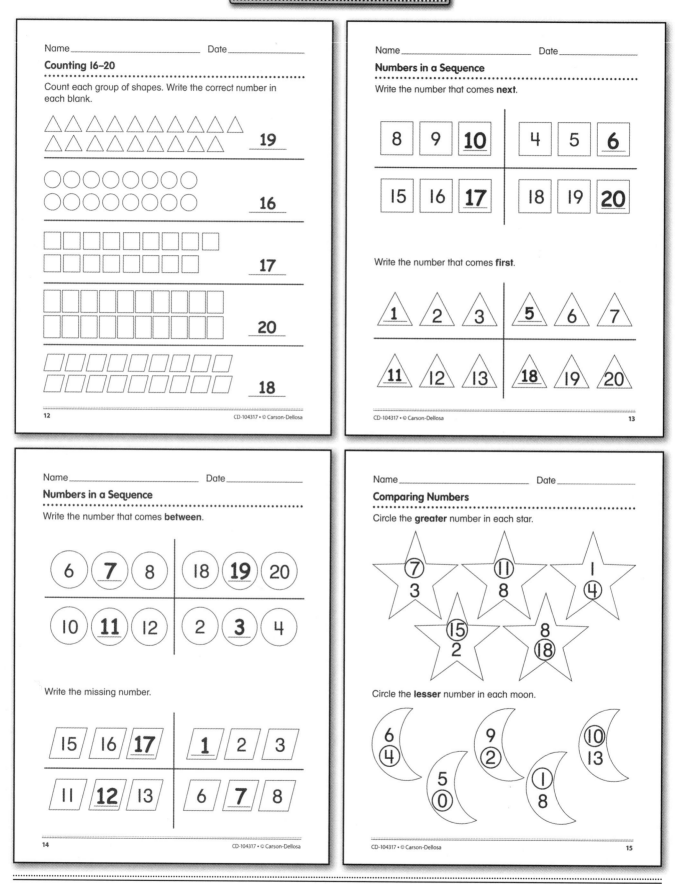

Name_____ Date_____

Counting 16–20

Count each group of shapes. Write the correct number in each blank.

△△△△△△△△
△△△△△△△ **19**

○○○○○○○○
○○○○○○○○ **16**

▢▢▢▢▢▢▢▢▢
▢▢▢▢▢▢▢▢ **17**

▢▢▢▢▢▢▢▢▢▢
▢▢▢▢▢▢▢▢▢▢ **20**

▱▱▱▱▱▱▱▱▱
▱▱▱▱▱▱▱▱▱ **18**

12   CD-104317 • © Carson-Dellosa

Name_____ Date_____

Numbers in a Sequence

Write the number that comes **next**.

| 8 | 9 | **10** | | 4 | 5 | **6** |

| 15 | 16 | **17** | | 18 | 19 | **20** |

Write the number that comes **first**.

△**1** △2 △3 | △**5** △6 △7

△**11** △12 △13 | △**18** △19 △20

CD-104317 • © Carson-Dellosa   13

Name_____ Date_____

Numbers in a Sequence

Write the number that comes **between**.

6 **7** 8 | 18 **19** 20

10 **11** 12 | 2 **3** 4

Write the missing number.

| 15 | 16 | **17** | | **1** | 2 | 3 |

| 11 | **12** | 13 | | 6 | **7** | 8 |

14   CD-104317 • © Carson-Dellosa

Name_____ Date_____

Comparing Numbers

Circle the **greater** number in each star.

⑦ / 3   ⑪ / 8   1 / ④

⑮ / 2   8 / ⑱

Circle the **lesser** number in each moon.

6 / ④   9 / ②   ⑩ / 13

5 / ⓪   1 / ⑧

CD-104317 • © Carson-Dellosa   15

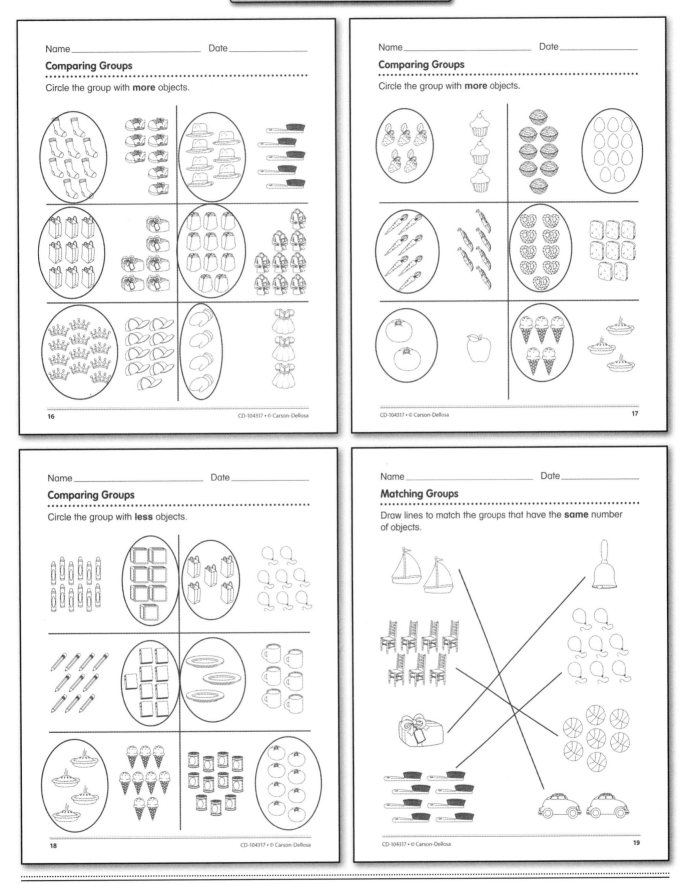

Name_____ Date_____

Comparing Groups

Circle the group with **more** objects.

16   CD-104317 • © Carson-Dellosa

Name_____ Date_____

Comparing Groups

Circle the group with **more** objects.

CD-104317 • © Carson-Dellosa   17

Name_____ Date_____

Comparing Groups

Circle the group with **less** objects.

18   CD-104317 • © Carson-Dellosa

Name_____ Date_____

Matching Groups

Draw lines to match the groups that have the **same** number of objects.

CD-104317 • © Carson-Dellosa   19

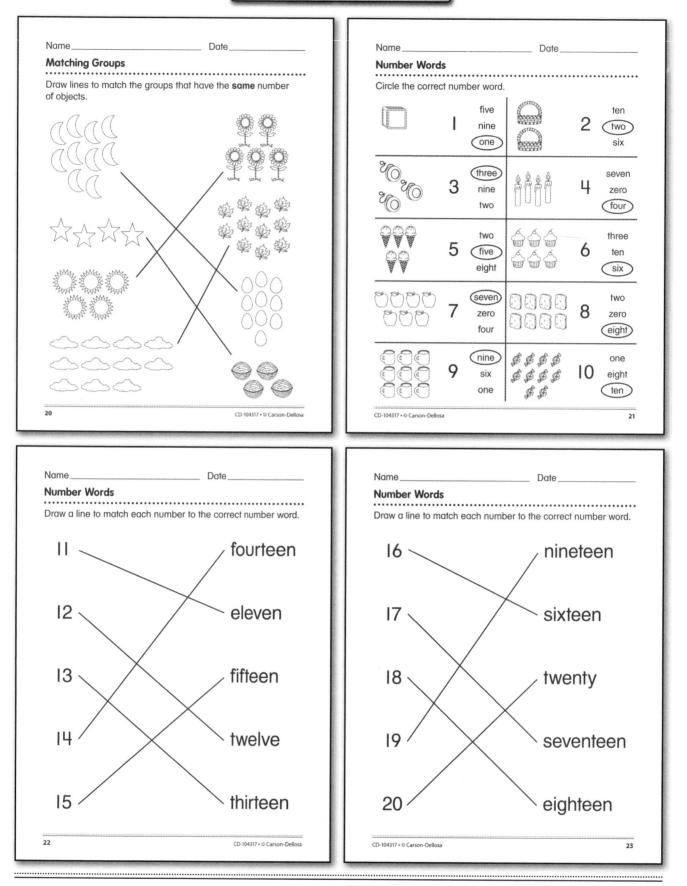

Name _____ Date _____

Matching Groups

Draw lines to match the groups that have the **same** number of objects.

20   CD-104317 • © Carson-Dellosa

Name _____ Date _____

Number Words

Circle the correct number word.

	1	five / nine / (one)	2	ten / (two) / six
	3	(three) / nine / two	4	seven / zero / (four)
	5	two / (five) / eight	6	three / ten / (six)
	7	(seven) / zero / four	8	two / zero / (eight)
	9	(nine) / six / one	10	one / eight / (ten)

CD-104317 • © Carson-Dellosa   21

Name _____ Date _____

Number Words

Draw a line to match each number to the correct number word.

11   fourteen

12   eleven

13   fifteen

14   twelve

15   thirteen

22   CD-104317 • © Carson-Dellosa

Name _____ Date _____

Number Words

Draw a line to match each number to the correct number word.

16   nineteen

17   sixteen

18   twenty

19   seventeen

20   eighteen

CD-104317 • © Carson-Dellosa   23

Name_____ Date_____

Ordinal Numbers

Circle the ordinal number that names the position of each item below.

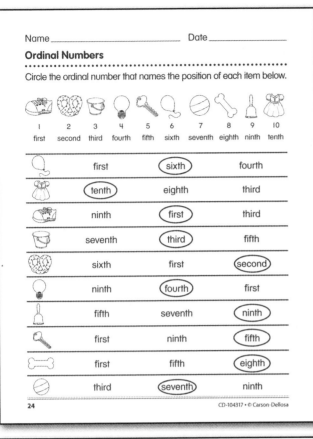

🎈	first	(sixth)	fourth
👗	(tenth)	eighth	third
👟	ninth	(first)	third
🪣	seventh	(third)	fifth
🥨	sixth	first	(second)
💡	ninth	(fourth)	first
🔔	fifth	seventh	(ninth)
🔑	first	ninth	(fifth)
🦴	first	fifth	(eighth)
⚾	third	(seventh)	ninth

24 CD-104317 • © Carson-Dellosa

Name_____ Date_____

Even Numbers

Numbers that end in 0, 2, 4, 6, or 8 are even numbers.
Even numbers can be divided into two equal groups.
Circle the **even numbers** in each row.

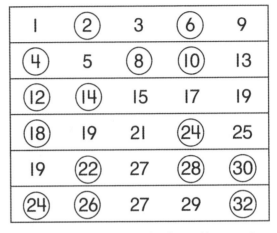

1	(2)	3	(6)	9
(4)	5	(8)	(10)	13
(12)	(14)	15	17	19
(18)	19	21	(24)	25
19	(22)	27	(28)	(30)
(24)	(26)	27	29	(32)

In each blank, write the **even number** that would come next.

2, 4, __6__, 8, __10__, 12, 14, 16, __18__

CD-104317 • © Carson-Dellosa 25

Name_____ Date_____

Odd Numbers

Numbers that end in 1, 3, 5, 7, or 9 are odd numbers.
Odd numbers cannot be divided into two equal groups.
Circle the **odd numbers** in each row.

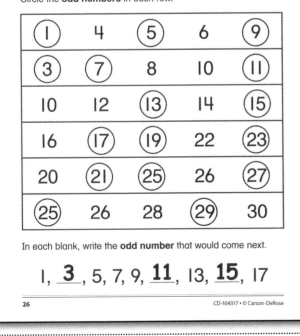

(1)	4	(5)	6	(9)
(3)	(7)	8	10	(11)
10	12	(13)	14	(15)
16	(17)	(19)	22	(23)
20	(21)	(25)	26	(27)
(25)	26	28	(29)	30

In each blank, write the **odd number** that would come next.

1, __3__, 5, 7, 9, __11__, 13, __15__, 17

26 CD-104317 • © Carson-Dellosa

Name_____ Date_____

Counting by 2s

On each number line, place a dot on the first even number.
Then, skip count by 2s. Place a dot on each number in
the pattern.

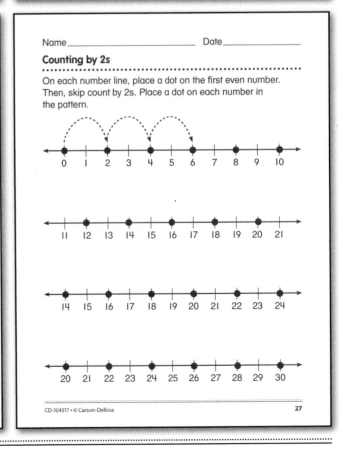

CD-104317 • © Carson-Dellosa 27

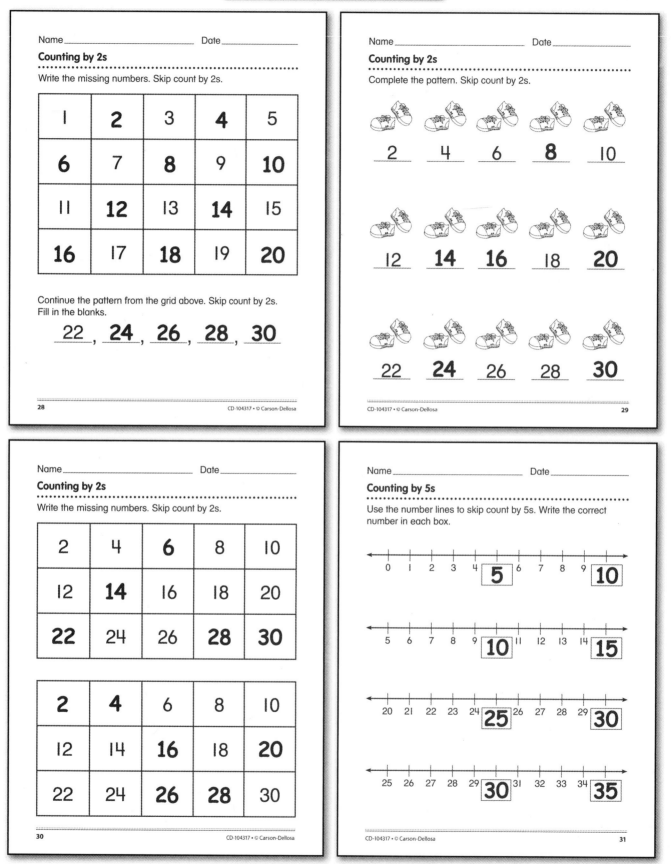

Name_____ Date_____

Counting by 2s

Write the missing numbers. Skip count by 2s.

1	**2**	3	**4**	5
6	7	**8**	9	**10**
11	**12**	13	**14**	15
16	17	**18**	19	**20**

Continue the pattern from the grid above. Skip count by 2s.
Fill in the blanks.

22, **24**, **26**, **28**, **30**

28 CD-104317 • © Carson-Dellosa

Name_____ Date_____

Counting by 2s

Complete the pattern. Skip count by 2s.

2 4 6 **8** 10

12 **14** **16** 18 **20**

22 **24** 26 28 **30**

CD-104317 • © Carson-Dellosa 29

Name_____ Date_____

Counting by 2s

Write the missing numbers. Skip count by 2s.

2	4	**6**	8	10
12	**14**	16	18	20
22	24	26	**28**	**30**

2	**4**	6	8	10
12	14	**16**	18	**20**
22	24	**26**	**28**	30

30 CD-104317 • © Carson-Dellosa

Name_____ Date_____

Counting by 5s

Use the number lines to skip count by 5s. Write the correct number in each box.

0 1 2 3 4 **5** 6 7 8 9 **10**

5 6 7 8 9 **10** 11 12 13 14 **15**

20 21 22 23 24 **25** 26 27 28 29 **30**

25 26 27 28 29 **30** 31 32 33 34 **35**

CD-104317 • © Carson-Dellosa 31

---

110   CD-104317 • © Carson-Dellosa

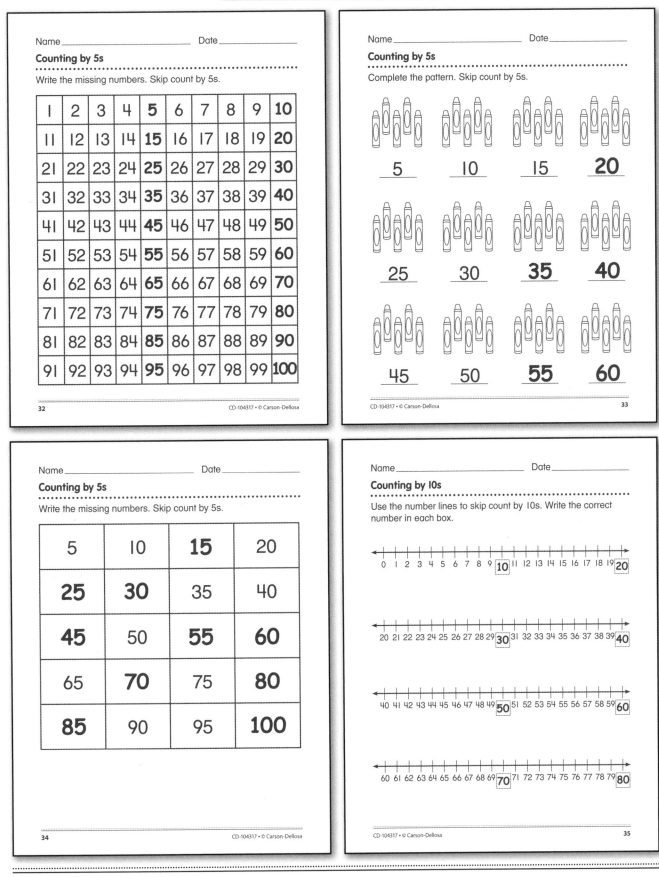

Name _____ Date _____

Counting by 5s

Write the missing numbers. Skip count by 5s.

1	2	3	4	**5**	6	7	8	9	**10**
11	12	13	14	**15**	16	17	18	19	**20**
21	22	23	24	**25**	26	27	28	29	**30**
31	32	33	34	**35**	36	37	38	39	**40**
41	42	43	44	**45**	46	47	48	49	**50**
51	52	53	54	**55**	56	57	58	59	**60**
61	62	63	64	**65**	66	67	68	69	**70**
71	72	73	74	**75**	76	77	78	79	**80**
81	82	83	84	**85**	86	87	88	89	**90**
91	92	93	94	**95**	96	97	98	99	**100**

32   CD-104317 • © Carson-Dellosa

Name _____ Date _____

Counting by 5s

Complete the pattern. Skip count by 5s.

5 _____ 10 _____ 15 _____ **20**

25 _____ 30 _____ **35** _____ **40**

45 _____ 50 _____ **55** _____ **60**

CD-104317 • © Carson-Dellosa   33

Name _____ Date _____

Counting by 5s

Write the missing numbers. Skip count by 5s.

5	10	**15**	20
25	**30**	35	40
45	50	**55**	**60**
65	**70**	75	**80**
85	90	95	**100**

34   CD-104317 • © Carson-Dellosa

Name _____ Date _____

Counting by 10s

Use the number lines to skip count by 10s. Write the correct number in each box.

0 1 2 3 4 5 6 7 8 9 **10** 11 12 13 14 15 16 17 18 19 **20**

20 21 22 23 24 25 26 27 28 29 **30** 31 32 33 34 35 36 37 38 39 **40**

40 41 42 43 44 45 46 47 48 49 **50** 51 52 53 54 55 56 57 58 59 **60**

60 61 62 63 64 65 66 67 68 69 **70** 71 72 73 74 75 76 77 78 79 **80**

CD-104317 • © Carson-Dellosa   35

Counting by 10s

Write the missing numbers. Skip count by 10s.

1	2	3	4	5	6	7	8	9	**10**
11	12	13	14	15	16	17	18	19	**20**
21	22	23	24	25	26	27	28	29	**30**
31	32	33	34	35	36	37	38	39	**40**
41	42	43	44	45	46	47	48	49	**50**
51	52	53	54	55	56	57	58	59	**60**
61	62	63	64	65	66	67	68	69	**70**
71	72	73	74	75	76	77	78	79	**80**
81	82	83	84	85	86	87	88	89	**90**
91	92	93	94	95	96	97	98	99	**100**

Counting by 10s

Complete the pattern. Skip count by 10s.

10	**20**	30	**40**
50	60	70	**80**
90	100	**110**	120

Counting by 10s

Write the missing numbers. Skip count by 10s.

10	**20**	**30**	40	50
60	**70**	80	**90**	100

10	20	30	**40**	50
60	**70**	80	90	**100**

Sums to 6

Total Problems:	15
Problems Correct:	_____

Solve each problem.

1. $\begin{array}{r} 1 \\ +5 \\ \hline 6 \end{array}$ 2. $\begin{array}{r} 2 \\ +0 \\ \hline 2 \end{array}$ 3. $\begin{array}{r} 3 \\ +1 \\ \hline 4 \end{array}$ 4. $\begin{array}{r} 3 \\ +3 \\ \hline 6 \end{array}$ 5. $\begin{array}{r} 3 \\ +2 \\ \hline 5 \end{array}$

6. $\begin{array}{r} 1 \\ +2 \\ \hline 3 \end{array}$ 7. $\begin{array}{r} 6 \\ +0 \\ \hline 6 \end{array}$ 8. $\begin{array}{r} 2 \\ +2 \\ \hline 4 \end{array}$ 9. $\begin{array}{r} 4 \\ +0 \\ \hline 4 \end{array}$ 10. $\begin{array}{r} 2 \\ +3 \\ \hline 5 \end{array}$

11. $\begin{array}{r} 1 \\ +1 \\ \hline 2 \end{array}$ 12. $\begin{array}{r} 2 \\ +4 \\ \hline 6 \end{array}$ 13. $\begin{array}{r} 1 \\ +0 \\ \hline 1 \end{array}$ 14. $\begin{array}{r} 2 \\ +1 \\ \hline 3 \end{array}$ 15. $\begin{array}{r} 1 \\ +3 \\ \hline 4 \end{array}$

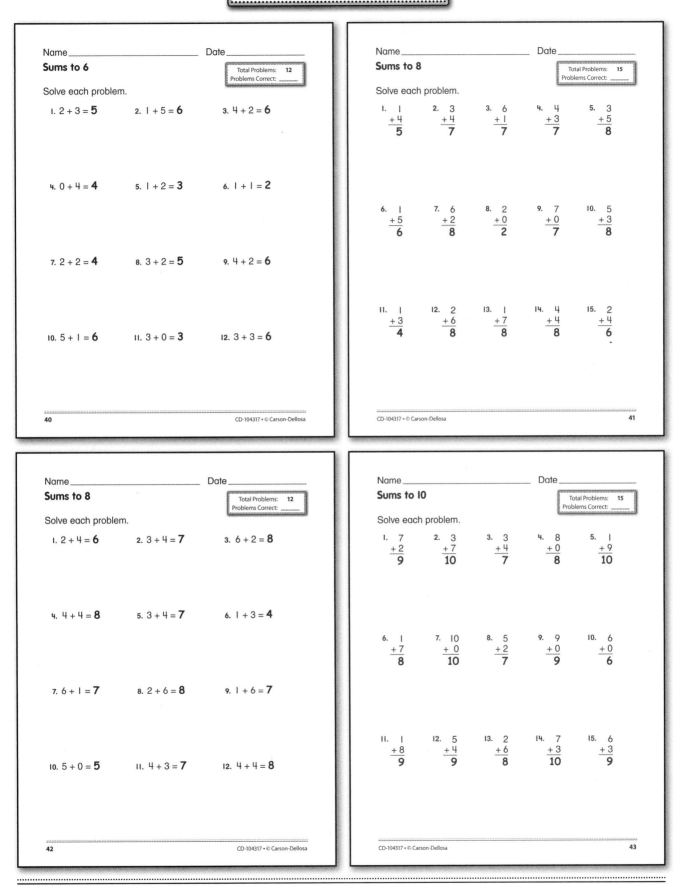

Name_____ Date_____

Sums to 6

| Total Problems: | 12 |
| Problems Correct: | _____ |

Solve each problem.

1. $2 + 3 = $ **5**   2. $1 + 5 = $ **6**   3. $4 + 2 = $ **6**

4. $0 + 4 = $ **4**   5. $1 + 2 = $ **3**   6. $1 + 1 = $ **2**

7. $2 + 2 = $ **4**   8. $3 + 2 = $ **5**   9. $4 + 2 = $ **6**

10. $5 + 1 = $ **6**   11. $3 + 0 = $ **3**   12. $3 + 3 = $ **6**

40   CD-104317 • © Carson-Dellosa

Name_____ Date_____

Sums to 8

| Total Problems: | 15 |
| Problems Correct: | _____ |

Solve each problem.

1. $\begin{array}{r} 1 \\ +4 \\ \hline 5 \end{array}$ 2. $\begin{array}{r} 3 \\ +4 \\ \hline 7 \end{array}$ 3. $\begin{array}{r} 6 \\ +1 \\ \hline 7 \end{array}$ 4. $\begin{array}{r} 4 \\ +3 \\ \hline 7 \end{array}$ 5. $\begin{array}{r} 3 \\ +5 \\ \hline 8 \end{array}$

6. $\begin{array}{r} 1 \\ +5 \\ \hline 6 \end{array}$ 7. $\begin{array}{r} 6 \\ +2 \\ \hline 8 \end{array}$ 8. $\begin{array}{r} 2 \\ +0 \\ \hline 2 \end{array}$ 9. $\begin{array}{r} 7 \\ +0 \\ \hline 7 \end{array}$ 10. $\begin{array}{r} 5 \\ +3 \\ \hline 8 \end{array}$

11. $\begin{array}{r} 1 \\ +3 \\ \hline 4 \end{array}$ 12. $\begin{array}{r} 2 \\ +6 \\ \hline 8 \end{array}$ 13. $\begin{array}{r} 1 \\ +7 \\ \hline 8 \end{array}$ 14. $\begin{array}{r} 4 \\ +4 \\ \hline 8 \end{array}$ 15. $\begin{array}{r} 2 \\ +4 \\ \hline 6 \end{array}$

CD-104317 • © Carson-Dellosa   41

Name_____ Date_____

Sums to 8

| Total Problems: | 12 |
| Problems Correct: | _____ |

Solve each problem.

1. $2 + 4 = $ **6**   2. $3 + 4 = $ **7**   3. $6 + 2 = $ **8**

4. $4 + 4 = $ **8**   5. $3 + 4 = $ **7**   6. $1 + 3 = $ **4**

7. $6 + 1 = $ **7**   8. $2 + 6 = $ **8**   9. $1 + 6 = $ **7**

10. $5 + 0 = $ **5**   11. $4 + 3 = $ **7**   12. $4 + 4 = $ **8**

42   CD-104317 • © Carson-Dellosa

Name_____ Date_____

Sums to 10

| Total Problems: | 15 |
| Problems Correct: | _____ |

Solve each problem.

1. $\begin{array}{r} 7 \\ +2 \\ \hline 9 \end{array}$ 2. $\begin{array}{r} 3 \\ +7 \\ \hline 10 \end{array}$ 3. $\begin{array}{r} 3 \\ +4 \\ \hline 7 \end{array}$ 4. $\begin{array}{r} 8 \\ +0 \\ \hline 8 \end{array}$ 5. $\begin{array}{r} 1 \\ +9 \\ \hline 10 \end{array}$

6. $\begin{array}{r} 1 \\ +7 \\ \hline 8 \end{array}$ 7. $\begin{array}{r} 10 \\ +0 \\ \hline 10 \end{array}$ 8. $\begin{array}{r} 5 \\ +2 \\ \hline 7 \end{array}$ 9. $\begin{array}{r} 9 \\ +0 \\ \hline 9 \end{array}$ 10. $\begin{array}{r} 6 \\ +0 \\ \hline 6 \end{array}$

11. $\begin{array}{r} 1 \\ +8 \\ \hline 9 \end{array}$ 12. $\begin{array}{r} 5 \\ +4 \\ \hline 9 \end{array}$ 13. $\begin{array}{r} 2 \\ +6 \\ \hline 8 \end{array}$ 14. $\begin{array}{r} 7 \\ +3 \\ \hline 10 \end{array}$ 15. $\begin{array}{r} 6 \\ +3 \\ \hline 9 \end{array}$

CD-104317 • © Carson-Dellosa   43

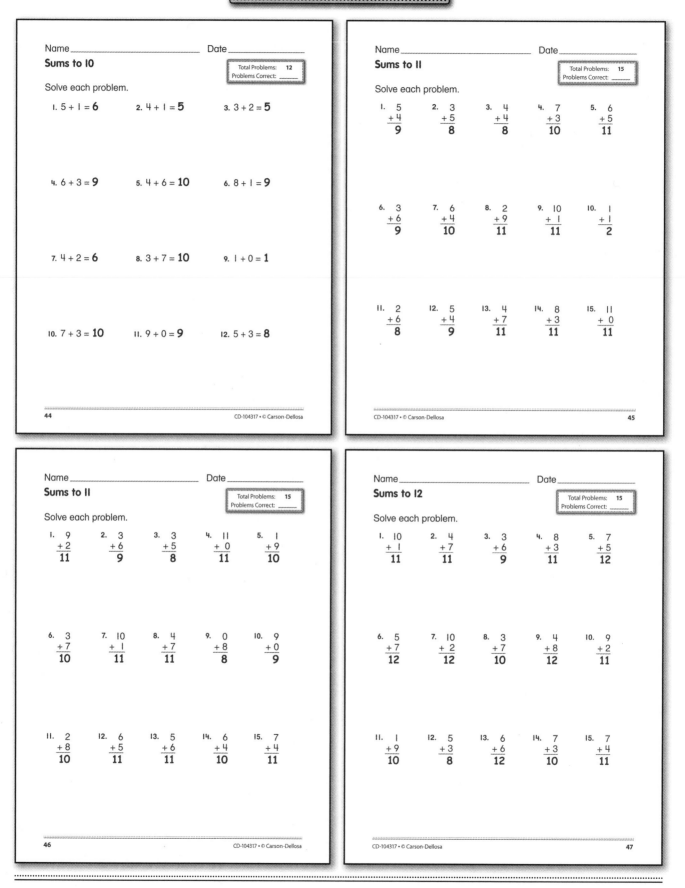

Name _____ Date _____

Sums to 10

Total Problems: **12**
Problems Correct: _____

Solve each problem.

1. $5 + 1 = $ **6**   2. $4 + 1 = $ **5**   3. $3 + 2 = $ **5**

4. $6 + 3 = $ **9**   5. $4 + 6 = $ **10**   6. $8 + 1 = $ **9**

7. $4 + 2 = $ **6**   8. $3 + 7 = $ **10**   9. $1 + 0 = $ **1**

10. $7 + 3 = $ **10**   11. $9 + 0 = $ **9**   12. $5 + 3 = $ **8**

44   CD-104317 • © Carson-Dellosa

Name _____ Date _____

Sums to 11

Total Problems: **15**
Problems Correct: _____

Solve each problem.

1.	2.	3.	4.	5.
5	3	4	7	6
+4	+5	+4	+3	+5
9	**8**	**8**	**10**	**11**

6.	7.	8.	9.	10.
3	6	2	10	1
+6	+4	+9	+1	+1
9	**10**	**11**	**11**	**2**

11.	12.	13.	14.	15.
2	5	4	8	11
+6	+4	+7	+3	+0
8	**9**	**11**	**11**	**11**

CD-104317 • © Carson-Dellosa   45

Name _____ Date _____

Sums to 11

Total Problems: **15**
Problems Correct: _____

Solve each problem.

1.	2.	3.	4.	5.
9	3	3	11	1
+2	+6	+5	+0	+9
11	**9**	**8**	**11**	**10**

6.	7.	8.	9.	10.
3	10	4	0	9
+7	+1	+7	+8	+0
10	**11**	**11**	**8**	**9**

11.	12.	13.	14.	15.
2	6	5	6	7
+8	+5	+6	+4	+4
10	**11**	**11**	**10**	**11**

46   CD-104317 • © Carson-Dellosa

Name _____ Date _____

Sums to 12

Total Problems: **15**
Problems Correct: _____

Solve each problem.

1.	2.	3.	4.	5.
10	4	3	8	7
+1	+7	+6	+3	+5
11	**11**	**9**	**11**	**12**

6.	7.	8.	9.	10.
5	10	3	4	9
+7	+2	+7	+8	+2
12	**12**	**10**	**12**	**11**

11.	12.	13.	14.	15.
1	5	6	7	7
+9	+3	+6	+3	+4
10	**8**	**12**	**10**	**11**

CD-104317 • © Carson-Dellosa   47

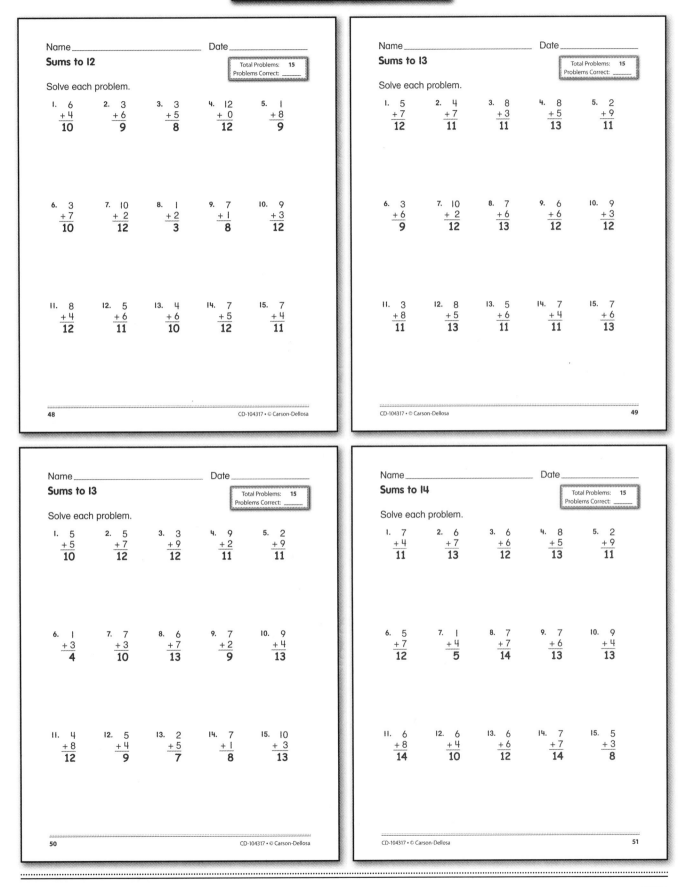

Name _____ Date _____

Sums to 12

Total Problems: 15
Problems Correct: _____

Solve each problem.

1. 6 +4 = **10**	2. 3 +6 = **9**	3. 3 +5 = **8**	4. 12 +0 = **12**	5. 1 +8 = **9**
6. 3 +7 = **10**	7. 10 +2 = **12**	8. 1 +2 = **3**	9. 7 +1 = **8**	10. 9 +3 = **12**
11. 8 +4 = **12**	12. 5 +6 = **11**	13. 4 +6 = **10**	14. 7 +5 = **12**	15. 7 +4 = **11**

CD-104317 • © Carson-Dellosa

Name _____ Date _____

Sums to 13

Total Problems: 15
Problems Correct: _____

Solve each problem.

1. 5 +7 = **12**	2. 4 +7 = **11**	3. 8 +3 = **11**	4. 8 +5 = **13**	5. 2 +9 = **11**
6. 3 +6 = **9**	7. 10 +2 = **12**	8. 7 +6 = **13**	9. 6 +6 = **12**	10. 9 +3 = **12**
11. 3 +8 = **11**	12. 8 +5 = **13**	13. 5 +6 = **11**	14. 7 +4 = **11**	15. 7 +6 = **13**

CD-104317 • © Carson-Dellosa

Name _____ Date _____

Sums to 13

Total Problems: 15
Problems Correct: _____

Solve each problem.

1. 5 +5 = **10**	2. 5 +7 = **12**	3. 3 +9 = **12**	4. 9 +2 = **11**	5. 2 +9 = **11**
6. 1 +3 = **4**	7. 7 +3 = **10**	8. 6 +7 = **13**	9. 7 +2 = **9**	10. 9 +4 = **13**
11. 4 +8 = **12**	12. 5 +4 = **9**	13. 2 +5 = **7**	14. 7 +1 = **8**	15. 10 +3 = **13**

CD-104317 • © Carson-Dellosa

Name _____ Date _____

Sums to 14

Total Problems: 15
Problems Correct: _____

Solve each problem.

1. 7 +4 = **11**	2. 6 +7 = **13**	3. 6 +6 = **12**	4. 8 +5 = **13**	5. 2 +9 = **11**
6. 5 +7 = **12**	7. 1 +4 = **5**	8. 7 +7 = **14**	9. 7 +6 = **13**	10. 9 +4 = **13**
11. 6 +8 = **14**	12. 6 +4 = **10**	13. 6 +6 = **12**	14. 7 +7 = **14**	15. 5 +3 = **8**

CD-104317 • © Carson-Dellosa

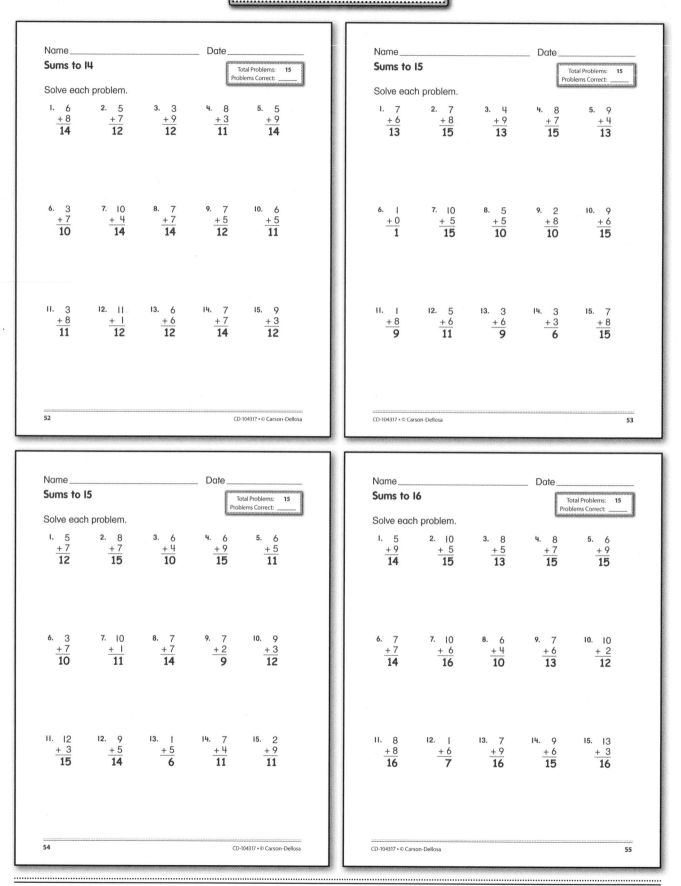

Name _____ Date _____

Sums to 14

Total Problems: **15**
Problems Correct: _____

Solve each problem.

1. 6
   +8
   14

2. 5
   +7
   12

3. 3
   +9
   12

4. 8
   +3
   11

5. 5
   +9
   14

6. 3
   +7
   10

7. 10
   +4
   14

8. 7
   +7
   14

9. 7
   +5
   12

10. 6
    +5
    11

11. 3
    +8
    11

12. 11
    +1
    12

13. 6
    +6
    12

14. 7
    +7
    14

15. 9
    +3
    12

52   CD-104317 • © Carson-Dellosa

Name _____ Date _____

Sums to 15

Total Problems: **15**
Problems Correct: _____

Solve each problem.

1. 7
   +6
   13

2. 7
   +8
   15

3. 4
   +9
   13

4. 8
   +7
   15

5. 9
   +4
   13

6. 1
   +0
   1

7. 10
   +5
   15

8. 5
   +5
   10

9. 2
   +8
   10

10. 9
    +6
    15

11. 1
    +8
    9

12. 5
    +6
    11

13. 3
    +6
    9

14. 3
    +3
    6

15. 7
    +8
    15

CD-104317 • © Carson-Dellosa   53

Name _____ Date _____

Sums to 15

Total Problems: **15**
Problems Correct: _____

Solve each problem.

1. 5
   +7
   12

2. 8
   +7
   15

3. 6
   +4
   10

4. 6
   +9
   15

5. 6
   +5
   11

6. 3
   +7
   10

7. 10
   +1
   11

8. 7
   +7
   14

9. 7
   +2
   9

10. 9
    +3
    12

11. 12
    +3
    15

12. 9
    +5
    14

13. 1
    +5
    6

14. 7
    +4
    11

15. 2
    +9
    11

54   CD-104317 • © Carson-Dellosa

Name _____ Date _____

Sums to 16

Total Problems: **15**
Problems Correct: _____

Solve each problem.

1. 5
   +9
   14

2. 10
   +5
   15

3. 8
   +5
   13

4. 8
   +7
   15

5. 6
   +9
   15

6. 7
   +7
   14

7. 10
   +6
   16

8. 6
   +4
   10

9. 7
   +6
   13

10. 10
    +2
    12

11. 8
    +8
    16

12. 1
    +6
    7

13. 7
    +9
    16

14. 9
    +6
    15

15. 13
    +3
    16

CD-104317 • © Carson-Dellosa   55

Name_____ Date_____

Sums to 16

Total Problems: 15
Problems Correct: _____

Solve each problem.

| 1. | 11
 + 5
 16 | 2. | 8
 + 7
 15 | 3. | 7
 + 9
 16 | 4. | 12
 + 4
 16 | 5. | 5
 + 5
 10 |

| 6. | 6
 + 8
 14 | 7. | 11
 + 2
 13 | 8. | 13
 + 2
 15 | 9. | 4
 + 2
 6 | 10. | 10
 + 6
 16 |

| 11. | 6
 + 7
 13 | 12. | 5
 + 6
 11 | 13. | 9
 + 5
 14 | 14. | 2
 + 8
 10 | 15. | 9
 + 3
 12 |

56 CD-104317 • © Carson-Dellosa

Name_____ Date_____

Sums to 17

Total Problems: 15
Problems Correct: _____

Solve each problem.

| 1. | 15
 + 1
 16 | 2. | 4
 + 7
 11 | 3. | 9
 + 4
 13 | 4. | 10
 + 7
 17 | 5. | 5
 + 8
 13 |

| 6. | 4
 + 6
 10 | 7. | 14
 + 3
 17 | 8. | 8
 + 9
 17 | 9. | 3
 + 8
 11 | 10. | 11
 + 4
 15 |

| 11. | 13
 + 3
 16 | 12. | 5
 + 9
 14 | 13. | 9
 + 8
 17 | 14. | 4
 + 4
 8 | 15. | 15
 + 2
 17 |

CD-104317 • © Carson-Dellosa 57

Name_____ Date_____

Sums to 17

Total Problems: 15
Problems Correct: _____

Solve each problem.

| 1. | 7
 + 6
 13 | 2. | 10
 + 3
 13 | 3. | 7
 + 7
 14 | 4. | 13
 + 4
 17 | 5. | 15
 + 1
 16 |

| 6. | 8
 + 7
 15 | 7. | 11
 + 4
 15 | 8. | 9
 + 5
 14 | 9. | 11
 + 6
 17 | 10. | 12
 + 5
 17 |

| 11. | 10
 + 7
 17 | 12. | 1
 + 7
 8 | 13. | 7
 + 9
 16 | 14. | 10
 + 0
 10 | 15. | 9
 + 4
 13 |

58 CD-104317 • © Carson-Dellosa

Name_____ Date_____

Sums to 18

Total Problems: 15
Problems Correct: _____

Solve each problem.

| 1. | 13
 + 4
 17 | 2. | 8
 + 7
 15 | 3. | 4
 + 9
 13 | 4. | 6
 + 9
 15 | 5. | 11
 + 5
 16 |

| 6. | 12
 + 1
 13 | 7. | 10
 + 8
 18 | 8. | 9
 + 5
 14 | 9. | 4
 + 7
 11 | 10. | 10
 + 2
 12 |

| 11. | 10
 + 4
 14 | 12. | 14
 + 4
 18 | 13. | 12
 + 5
 17 | 14. | 15
 + 2
 17 | 15. | 9
 + 2
 11 |

CD-104317 • © Carson-Dellosa 59

Name _____ Date _____

Sums to 18

Total Problems: 15
Problems Correct: _____

Solve each problem.

| 1. $\begin{array}{r} 1 \\ +8 \\ \hline 9 \end{array}$ | 2. $\begin{array}{r} 15 \\ +3 \\ \hline 18 \end{array}$ | 3. $\begin{array}{r} 10 \\ +8 \\ \hline 18 \end{array}$ | 4. $\begin{array}{r} 12 \\ +4 \\ \hline 16 \end{array}$ | 5. $\begin{array}{r} 8 \\ +9 \\ \hline 17 \end{array}$ |

| 6. $\begin{array}{r} 9 \\ +3 \\ \hline 12 \end{array}$ | 7. $\begin{array}{r} 11 \\ +2 \\ \hline 13 \end{array}$ | 8. $\begin{array}{r} 11 \\ +7 \\ \hline 18 \end{array}$ | 9. $\begin{array}{r} 12 \\ +5 \\ \hline 17 \end{array}$ | 10. $\begin{array}{r} 8 \\ +2 \\ \hline 10 \end{array}$ |

| 11. $\begin{array}{r} 8 \\ +5 \\ \hline 13 \end{array}$ | 12. $\begin{array}{r} 9 \\ +9 \\ \hline 18 \end{array}$ | 13. $\begin{array}{r} 7 \\ +6 \\ \hline 13 \end{array}$ | 14. $\begin{array}{r} 9 \\ +7 \\ \hline 16 \end{array}$ | 15. $\begin{array}{r} 13 \\ +5 \\ \hline 18 \end{array}$ |

60   CD-104317 • © Carson-Dellosa

Name _____ Date _____

Differences from 6 or Less

Total Problems: 15
Problems Correct: _____

Solve each problem.

| 1. $\begin{array}{r} 2 \\ -0 \\ \hline 2 \end{array}$ | 2. $\begin{array}{r} 5 \\ -5 \\ \hline 0 \end{array}$ | 3. $\begin{array}{r} 3 \\ -1 \\ \hline 2 \end{array}$ | 4. $\begin{array}{r} 3 \\ -3 \\ \hline 0 \end{array}$ | 5. $\begin{array}{r} 3 \\ -2 \\ \hline 1 \end{array}$ |

| 6. $\begin{array}{r} 5 \\ -3 \\ \hline 2 \end{array}$ | 7. $\begin{array}{r} 6 \\ -0 \\ \hline 6 \end{array}$ | 8. $\begin{array}{r} 2 \\ -2 \\ \hline 0 \end{array}$ | 9. $\begin{array}{r} 4 \\ -0 \\ \hline 4 \end{array}$ | 10. $\begin{array}{r} 6 \\ -3 \\ \hline 3 \end{array}$ |

| 11. $\begin{array}{r} 1 \\ -1 \\ \hline 0 \end{array}$ | 12. $\begin{array}{r} 5 \\ -4 \\ \hline 1 \end{array}$ | 13. $\begin{array}{r} 1 \\ -0 \\ \hline 1 \end{array}$ | 14. $\begin{array}{r} 4 \\ -1 \\ \hline 3 \end{array}$ | 15. $\begin{array}{r} 3 \\ -3 \\ \hline 0 \end{array}$ |

CD-104317 • © Carson-Dellosa   61

Name _____ Date _____

Differences from 6 or Less

Total Problems: 15
Problems Correct: _____

Solve each problem.

| 1. $\begin{array}{r} 6 \\ -3 \\ \hline 3 \end{array}$ | 2. $\begin{array}{r} 2 \\ -2 \\ \hline 0 \end{array}$ | 3. $\begin{array}{r} 1 \\ -1 \\ \hline 0 \end{array}$ | 4. $\begin{array}{r} 4 \\ -0 \\ \hline 4 \end{array}$ | 5. $\begin{array}{r} 4 \\ -2 \\ \hline 2 \end{array}$ |

| 6. $\begin{array}{r} 3 \\ -0 \\ \hline 3 \end{array}$ | 7. $\begin{array}{r} 0 \\ -0 \\ \hline 0 \end{array}$ | 8. $\begin{array}{r} 5 \\ -4 \\ \hline 1 \end{array}$ | 9. $\begin{array}{r} 4 \\ -1 \\ \hline 3 \end{array}$ | 10. $\begin{array}{r} 5 \\ -2 \\ \hline 3 \end{array}$ |

| 11. $\begin{array}{r} 6 \\ -4 \\ \hline 2 \end{array}$ | 12. $\begin{array}{r} 3 \\ -1 \\ \hline 2 \end{array}$ | 13. $\begin{array}{r} 6 \\ -2 \\ \hline 4 \end{array}$ | 14. $\begin{array}{r} 4 \\ -3 \\ \hline 1 \end{array}$ | 15. $\begin{array}{r} 5 \\ -1 \\ \hline 4 \end{array}$ |

62   CD-104317 • © Carson-Dellosa

Name _____ Date _____

Differences from 10 or Less

Total Problems: 15
Problems Correct: _____

Solve each problem.

| 1. $\begin{array}{r} 8 \\ -5 \\ \hline 3 \end{array}$ | 2. $\begin{array}{r} 9 \\ -4 \\ \hline 5 \end{array}$ | 3. $\begin{array}{r} 8 \\ -6 \\ \hline 2 \end{array}$ | 4. $\begin{array}{r} 10 \\ -3 \\ \hline 7 \end{array}$ | 5. $\begin{array}{r} 6 \\ -2 \\ \hline 4 \end{array}$ |

| 6. $\begin{array}{r} 9 \\ -3 \\ \hline 6 \end{array}$ | 7. $\begin{array}{r} 7 \\ -5 \\ \hline 2 \end{array}$ | 8. $\begin{array}{r} 6 \\ -4 \\ \hline 2 \end{array}$ | 9. $\begin{array}{r} 10 \\ -8 \\ \hline 2 \end{array}$ | 10. $\begin{array}{r} 4 \\ -2 \\ \hline 2 \end{array}$ |

| 11. $\begin{array}{r} 9 \\ -5 \\ \hline 4 \end{array}$ | 12. $\begin{array}{r} 7 \\ -6 \\ \hline 1 \end{array}$ | 13. $\begin{array}{r} 8 \\ -4 \\ \hline 4 \end{array}$ | 14. $\begin{array}{r} 10 \\ -3 \\ \hline 7 \end{array}$ | 15. $\begin{array}{r} 8 \\ -2 \\ \hline 6 \end{array}$ |

CD-104317 • © Carson-Dellosa   63

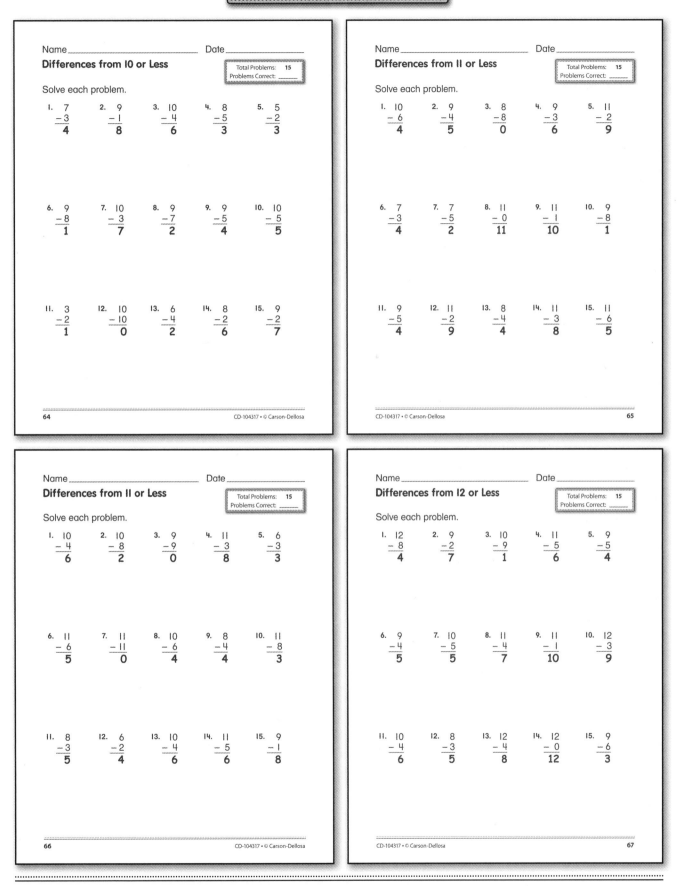

Name_____ Date_____

Differences from 10 or Less

Total Problems: 15
Problems Correct: _____

Solve each problem.

1. 7 − 3 **4**	2. 9 − 1 **8**	3. 10 − 4 **6**	4. 8 − 5 **3**	5. 5 − 2 **3**
6. 9 − 8 **1**	7. 10 − 3 **7**	8. 9 − 7 **2**	9. 9 − 5 **4**	10. 10 − 5 **5**
11. 3 − 2 **1**	12. 10 − 10 **0**	13. 6 − 4 **2**	14. 8 − 2 **6**	15. 9 − 2 **7**

64   CD-104317 • © Carson-Dellosa

Name_____ Date_____

Differences from 11 or Less

Total Problems: 15
Problems Correct: _____

Solve each problem.

1. 10 − 6 **4**	2. 9 − 4 **5**	3. 8 − 8 **0**	4. 9 − 3 **6**	5. 11 − 2 **9**
6. 7 − 3 **4**	7. 7 − 5 **2**	8. 11 − 0 **11**	9. 11 − 1 **10**	10. 9 − 8 **1**
11. 9 − 5 **4**	12. 11 − 2 **9**	13. 8 − 4 **4**	14. 11 − 3 **8**	15. 11 − 6 **5**

CD-104317 • © Carson-Dellosa   65

Name_____ Date_____

Differences from 11 or Less

Total Problems: 15
Problems Correct: _____

Solve each problem.

1. 10 − 4 **6**	2. 10 − 8 **2**	3. 9 − 9 **0**	4. 11 − 3 **8**	5. 6 − 3 **3**
6. 11 − 6 **5**	7. 11 − 11 **0**	8. 10 − 6 **4**	9. 8 − 4 **4**	10. 11 − 8 **3**
11. 8 − 3 **5**	12. 6 − 2 **4**	13. 10 − 4 **6**	14. 11 − 5 **6**	15. 9 − 1 **8**

66   CD-104317 • © Carson-Dellosa

Name_____ Date_____

Differences from 12 or Less

Total Problems: 15
Problems Correct: _____

Solve each problem.

1. 12 − 8 **4**	2. 9 − 2 **7**	3. 10 − 9 **1**	4. 11 − 5 **6**	5. 9 − 5 **4**
6. 9 − 4 **5**	7. 10 − 5 **5**	8. 11 − 4 **7**	9. 11 − 1 **10**	10. 12 − 3 **9**
11. 10 − 4 **6**	12. 8 − 3 **5**	13. 12 − 4 **8**	14. 12 − 0 **12**	15. 9 − 6 **3**

CD-104317 • © Carson-Dellosa   67

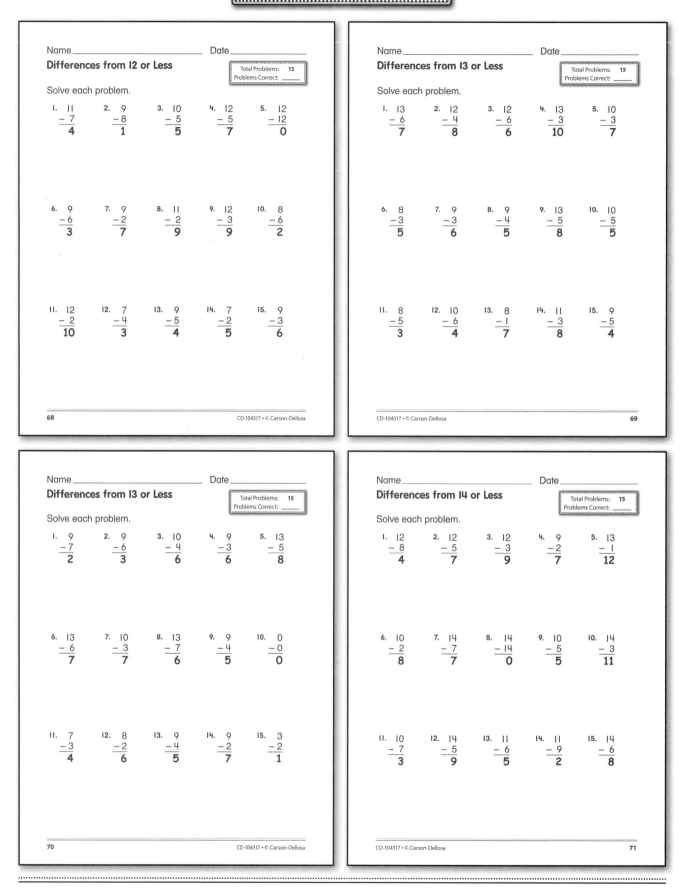

Worksheet 1 (page 68)

Name _____ Date _____

Differences from 12 or Less

Total Problems: 15
Problems Correct: _____

Solve each problem.

1. 11 − 7 = **4**	2. 9 − 8 = **1**	3. 10 − 5 = **5**	4. 12 − 5 = **7**	5. 12 − 12 = **0**
6. 9 − 6 = **3**	7. 9 − 2 = **7**	8. 11 − 2 = **9**	9. 12 − 3 = **9**	10. 8 − 6 = **2**
11. 12 − 2 = **10**	12. 7 − 4 = **3**	13. 9 − 5 = **4**	14. 7 − 2 = **5**	15. 9 − 3 = **6**

CD-104317 • © Carson-Dellosa

Worksheet 2 (page 69)

Name _____ Date _____

Differences from 13 or Less

Total Problems: 15
Problems Correct: _____

Solve each problem.

1. 13 − 6 = **7**	2. 12 − 4 = **8**	3. 12 − 6 = **6**	4. 13 − 3 = **10**	5. 10 − 3 = **7**
6. 8 − 3 = **5**	7. 9 − 3 = **6**	8. 9 − 4 = **5**	9. 13 − 5 = **8**	10. 10 − 5 = **5**
11. 8 − 5 = **3**	12. 10 − 6 = **4**	13. 8 − 1 = **7**	14. 11 − 3 = **8**	15. 9 − 5 = **4**

CD-104317 • © Carson-Dellosa

Worksheet 3 (page 70)

Name _____ Date _____

Differences from 13 or Less

Total Problems: 15
Problems Correct: _____

Solve each problem.

1. 9 − 7 = **2**	2. 9 − 6 = **3**	3. 10 − 4 = **6**	4. 9 − 3 = **6**	5. 13 − 5 = **8**
6. 13 − 6 = **7**	7. 10 − 3 = **7**	8. 13 − 7 = **6**	9. 9 − 4 = **5**	10. 0 − 0 = **0**
11. 7 − 3 = **4**	12. 8 − 2 = **6**	13. 9 − 4 = **5**	14. 9 − 2 = **7**	15. 3 − 2 = **1**

CD-104317 • © Carson-Dellosa

Worksheet 4 (page 71)

Name _____ Date _____

Differences from 14 or Less

Total Problems: 15
Problems Correct: _____

Solve each problem.

1. 12 − 8 = **4**	2. 12 − 5 = **7**	3. 12 − 3 = **9**	4. 9 − 2 = **7**	5. 13 − 1 = **12**
6. 10 − 2 = **8**	7. 14 − 7 = **7**	8. 14 − 14 = **0**	9. 10 − 5 = **5**	10. 14 − 3 = **11**
11. 10 − 7 = **3**	12. 14 − 5 = **9**	13. 11 − 6 = **5**	14. 11 − 9 = **2**	15. 14 − 6 = **8**

CD-104317 • © Carson-Dellosa

CD-104317 • © Carson-Dellosa

Name _____ **Date** _____

Differences from 14 or Less

Total Problems: 15
Problems Correct: _____

Solve each problem.

1. 10
    − 4
    ___
     6

2. 13
    − 8
    ___
     5

3. 14
    − 2
    ___
    12

4. 11
    − 8
    ___
     3

5. 10
    − 6
    ___
     4

6. 13
    − 5
    ___
     8

7.   9
    − 3
    ___
     6

8. 11
    − 5
    ___
     6

9.   9
    − 5
    ___
     4

10. 14
    − 6
    ___
     8

11. 12
    − 9
    ___
     3

12. 11
    − 7
    ___
     4

13. 14
    − 7
    ___
     7

14. 10
    − 8
    ___
     2

15. 12
    − 4
    ___
     8

72   CD-104317 • © Carson-Dellosa

Name _____ **Date** _____

Differences from 15 or Less

Total Problems: 15
Problems Correct: _____

Solve each problem.

1. 14
    − 4
    ___
    10

2. 12
    − 4
    ___
     8

3. 15
    − 3
    ___
    12

4. 14
    − 6
    ___
     8

5. 10
    − 3
    ___
     7

6. 15
    − 8
    ___
     7

7. 15
    − 5
    ___
    10

8. 13
    − 3
    ___
    10

9. 10
    − 5
    ___
     5

10. 11
    − 5
    ___
     6

11. 15
    − 2
    ___
    13

12. 11
    − 6
    ___
     5

13. 10
    − 1
    ___
     9

14. 11
    − 3
    ___
     8

15. 12
    − 6
    ___
     6

CD-104317 • © Carson-Dellosa   73

Name _____ **Date** _____

Differences from 15 or Less

Total Problems: 15
Problems Correct: _____

Solve each problem.

1. 15
    − 2
    ___
    13

2. 15
    − 6
    ___
     9

3. 13
    − 4
    ___
     9

4. 15
    − 3
    ___
    12

5. 10
    − 3
    ___
     7

6. 14
    − 6
    ___
     8

7. 12
    − 8
    ___
     4

8. 13
    − 5
    ___
     8

9. 15
    − 15
    ___
     0

10. 10
    − 8
    ___
     2

11. 12
    − 3
    ___
     9

12. 11
    − 2
    ___
     9

13. 11
    − 5
    ___
     6

14. 13
    − 6
    ___
     7

15. 10
    − 2
    ___
     8

74   CD-104317 • © Carson-Dellosa

Name _____ **Date** _____

Differences from 16 or Less

Total Problems: 15
Problems Correct: _____

Solve each problem.

1. 13
    − 2
    ___
    11

2. 13
    − 8
    ___
     5

3. 15
    − 9
    ___
     6

4. 12
    − 8
    ___
     4

5. 10
    − 6
    ___
     4

6. 16
    − 9
    ___
     7

7. 10
    − 7
    ___
     3

8. 13
    − 3
    ___
    10

9. 11
    − 5
    ___
     6

10. 11
    − 9
    ___
     2

11. 10
    − 8
    ___
     2

12. 12
    − 3
    ___
     9

13. 16
    − 5
    ___
    11

14. 16
    − 4
    ___
    12

15. 12
    − 2
    ___
    10

CD-104317 • © Carson-Dellosa   75

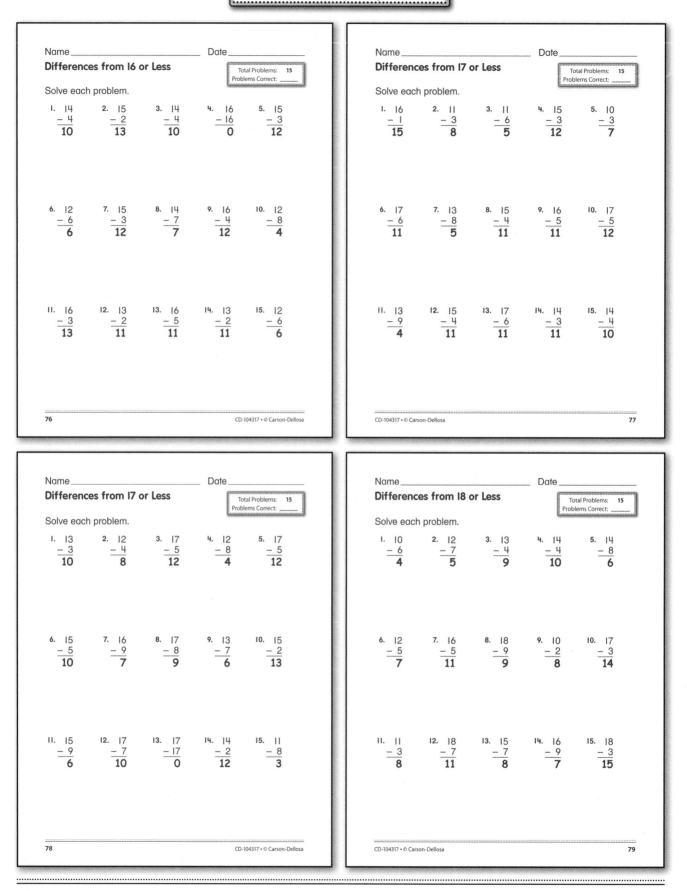

Name_____ Date_____

Differences from 16 or Less

Total Problems: **15**
Problems Correct: _____

Solve each problem.

1.	14 − 4 **10**	2.	15 − 2 **13**	3.	14 − 4 **10**	4.	16 − 16 **0**	5.	15 − 3 **12**

6.	12 − 6 **6**	7.	15 − 3 **12**	8.	14 − 7 **7**	9.	16 − 4 **12**	10.	12 − 8 **4**

11.	16 − 3 **13**	12.	13 − 2 **11**	13.	16 − 5 **11**	14.	13 − 2 **11**	15.	12 − 6 **6**

76   CD-104317 • © Carson-Dellosa

Name_____ Date_____

Differences from 17 or Less

Total Problems: **15**
Problems Correct: _____

Solve each problem.

1.	16 − 1 **15**	2.	11 − 3 **8**	3.	11 − 6 **5**	4.	15 − 3 **12**	5.	10 − 3 **7**

6.	17 − 6 **11**	7.	13 − 8 **5**	8.	15 − 4 **11**	9.	16 − 5 **11**	10.	17 − 5 **12**

11.	13 − 9 **4**	12.	15 − 4 **11**	13.	17 − 6 **11**	14.	14 − 3 **11**	15.	14 − 4 **10**

CD-104317 • © Carson-Dellosa   77

Name_____ Date_____

Differences from 17 or Less

Total Problems: **15**
Problems Correct: _____

Solve each problem.

1.	13 − 3 **10**	2.	12 − 4 **8**	3.	17 − 5 **12**	4.	12 − 8 **4**	5.	17 − 5 **12**

6.	15 − 5 **10**	7.	16 − 9 **7**	8.	17 − 8 **9**	9.	13 − 7 **6**	10.	15 − 2 **13**

11.	15 − 9 **6**	12.	17 − 7 **10**	13.	17 − 17 **0**	14.	14 − 2 **12**	15.	11 − 8 **3**

78   CD-104317 • © Carson-Dellosa

Name_____ Date_____

Differences from 18 or Less

Total Problems: **15**
Problems Correct: _____

Solve each problem.

1.	10 − 6 **4**	2.	12 − 7 **5**	3.	13 − 4 **9**	4.	14 − 4 **10**	5.	14 − 8 **6**

6.	12 − 5 **7**	7.	16 − 5 **11**	8.	18 − 9 **9**	9.	10 − 2 **8**	10.	17 − 3 **14**

11.	11 − 3 **8**	12.	18 − 7 **11**	13.	15 − 7 **8**	14.	16 − 9 **7**	15.	18 − 3 **15**

CD-104317 • © Carson-Dellosa   79

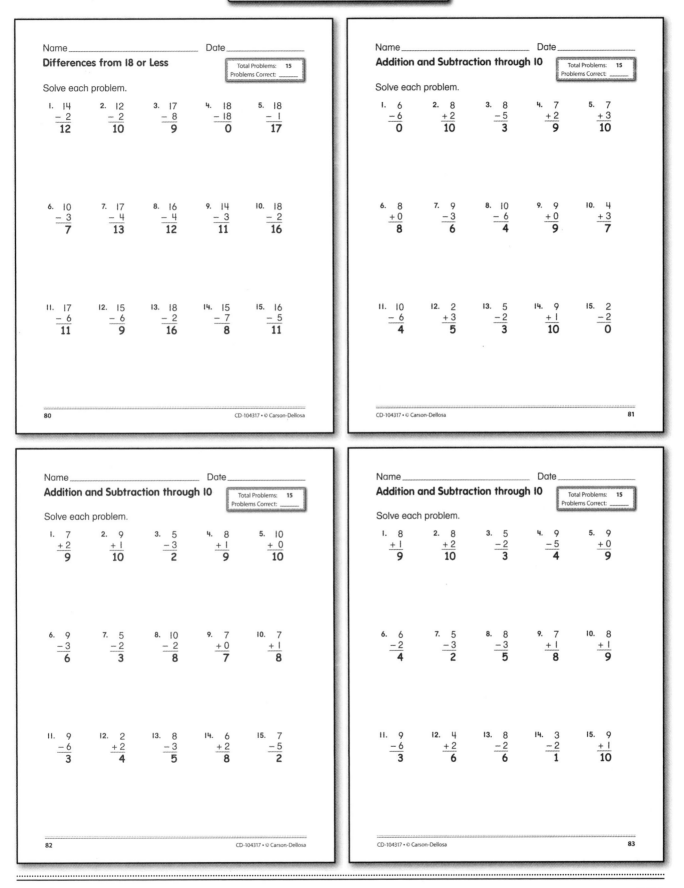

Name_____ Date_____

Differences from 18 or Less

Total Problems: 15
Problems Correct: _____

Solve each problem.

1. 14 − 2 **12**	2. 12 − 2 **10**	3. 17 − 8 **9**	4. 18 − 18 **0**	5. 18 − 1 **17**
6. 10 − 3 **7**	7. 17 − 4 **13**	8. 16 − 4 **12**	9. 14 − 3 **11**	10. 18 − 2 **16**
11. 17 − 6 **11**	12. 15 − 6 **9**	13. 18 − 2 **16**	14. 15 − 7 **8**	15. 16 − 5 **11**

CD-104317 • © Carson-Dellosa

Name_____ Date_____

Addition and Subtraction through 10

Total Problems: 15
Problems Correct: _____

Solve each problem.

1. 6 − 6 **0**	2. 8 + 2 **10**	3. 8 − 5 **3**	4. 7 + 2 **9**	5. 7 + 3 **10**
6. 8 + 0 **8**	7. 9 − 3 **6**	8. 10 − 6 **4**	9. 9 + 0 **9**	10. 4 + 3 **7**
11. 10 − 6 **4**	12. 2 + 3 **5**	13. 5 − 2 **3**	14. 9 + 1 **10**	15. 2 − 2 **0**

CD-104317 • © Carson-Dellosa

Name_____ Date_____

Addition and Subtraction through 10

Total Problems: 15
Problems Correct: _____

Solve each problem.

1. 7 + 2 **9**	2. 9 + 1 **10**	3. 5 − 3 **2**	4. 8 + 1 **9**	5. 10 + 0 **10**
6. 9 − 3 **6**	7. 5 − 2 **3**	8. 10 − 2 **8**	9. 7 + 0 **7**	10. 7 + 1 **8**
11. 9 − 6 **3**	12. 2 + 2 **4**	13. 8 − 3 **5**	14. 6 + 2 **8**	15. 7 − 5 **2**

CD-104317 • © Carson-Dellosa

Name_____ Date_____

Addition and Subtraction through 10

Total Problems: 15
Problems Correct: _____

Solve each problem.

1. 8 + 1 **9**	2. 8 + 2 **10**	3. 5 − 2 **3**	4. 9 − 5 **4**	5. 9 + 0 **9**
6. 6 − 2 **4**	7. 5 − 3 **2**	8. 8 − 3 **5**	9. 7 + 1 **8**	10. 8 + 1 **9**
11. 9 − 6 **3**	12. 4 + 2 **6**	13. 8 − 2 **6**	14. 3 − 2 **1**	15. 9 + 1 **10**

CD-104317 • © Carson-Dellosa

Name _____ Date _____

One-Digit Addition without Regrouping

Total Problems:	15
Problems Correct:	_____

Solve each problem.

1. $\begin{array}{r} 5 \\ +4 \\ \hline 9 \end{array}$
2. $\begin{array}{r} 7 \\ +0 \\ \hline 7 \end{array}$
3. $\begin{array}{r} 6 \\ +1 \\ \hline 7 \end{array}$
4. $\begin{array}{r} 3 \\ +1 \\ \hline 4 \end{array}$
5. $\begin{array}{r} 3 \\ +6 \\ \hline 9 \end{array}$

6. $\begin{array}{r} 4 \\ +4 \\ \hline 8 \end{array}$
7. $\begin{array}{r} 2 \\ +7 \\ \hline 9 \end{array}$
8. $\begin{array}{r} 8 \\ +1 \\ \hline 9 \end{array}$
9. $\begin{array}{r} 5 \\ +3 \\ \hline 8 \end{array}$
10. $\begin{array}{r} 7 \\ +1 \\ \hline 8 \end{array}$

11. $\begin{array}{r} 8 \\ +0 \\ \hline 8 \end{array}$
12. $\begin{array}{r} 6 \\ +2 \\ \hline 8 \end{array}$
13. $\begin{array}{r} 5 \\ +2 \\ \hline 7 \end{array}$
14. $\begin{array}{r} 4 \\ +3 \\ \hline 7 \end{array}$
15. $\begin{array}{r} 3 \\ +5 \\ \hline 8 \end{array}$

84   CD-104317 • © Carson-Dellosa

Name _____ Date _____

One-Digit Addition with Regrouping

Total Problems:	15
Problems Correct:	_____

Solve each problem.

1. $\begin{array}{r} 2 \\ +8 \\ \hline 10 \end{array}$
2. $\begin{array}{r} 7 \\ +8 \\ \hline 15 \end{array}$
3. $\begin{array}{r} 6 \\ +8 \\ \hline 14 \end{array}$
4. $\begin{array}{r} 6 \\ +5 \\ \hline 11 \end{array}$
5. $\begin{array}{r} 3 \\ +9 \\ \hline 12 \end{array}$

6. $\begin{array}{r} 4 \\ +7 \\ \hline 11 \end{array}$
7. $\begin{array}{r} 9 \\ +9 \\ \hline 18 \end{array}$
8. $\begin{array}{r} 8 \\ +5 \\ \hline 13 \end{array}$
9. $\begin{array}{r} 9 \\ +8 \\ \hline 17 \end{array}$
10. $\begin{array}{r} 7 \\ +6 \\ \hline 13 \end{array}$

11. $\begin{array}{r} 8 \\ +8 \\ \hline 16 \end{array}$
12. $\begin{array}{r} 6 \\ +7 \\ \hline 13 \end{array}$
13. $\begin{array}{r} 5 \\ +6 \\ \hline 11 \end{array}$
14. $\begin{array}{r} 4 \\ +7 \\ \hline 11 \end{array}$
15. $\begin{array}{r} 8 \\ +7 \\ \hline 15 \end{array}$

CD-104317 • © Carson-Dellosa   85

Name _____ Date _____

Two-Digit Addition without Regrouping

Total Problems:	15
Problems Correct:	_____

Solve each problem.

1. $\begin{array}{r} 15 \\ +4 \\ \hline 19 \end{array}$
2. $\begin{array}{r} 12 \\ +7 \\ \hline 19 \end{array}$
3. $\begin{array}{r} 17 \\ +1 \\ \hline 18 \end{array}$
4. $\begin{array}{r} 12 \\ +3 \\ \hline 15 \end{array}$
5. $\begin{array}{r} 10 \\ +5 \\ \hline 15 \end{array}$

6. $\begin{array}{r} 15 \\ +2 \\ \hline 17 \end{array}$
7. $\begin{array}{r} 11 \\ +8 \\ \hline 19 \end{array}$
8. $\begin{array}{r} 11 \\ +6 \\ \hline 17 \end{array}$
9. $\begin{array}{r} 13 \\ +5 \\ \hline 18 \end{array}$
10. $\begin{array}{r} 10 \\ +7 \\ \hline 17 \end{array}$

11. $\begin{array}{r} 10 \\ +2 \\ \hline 12 \end{array}$
12. $\begin{array}{r} 16 \\ +2 \\ \hline 18 \end{array}$
13. $\begin{array}{r} 14 \\ +3 \\ \hline 17 \end{array}$
14. $\begin{array}{r} 12 \\ +1 \\ \hline 13 \end{array}$
15. $\begin{array}{r} 14 \\ +4 \\ \hline 18 \end{array}$

86   CD-104317 • © Carson-Dellosa

Name _____ Date _____

Two-Digit Addition with Regrouping

Total Problems:	15
Problems Correct:	_____

Solve each problem.

1. $\begin{array}{r} 11 \\ +9 \\ \hline 20 \end{array}$
2. $\begin{array}{r} 14 \\ +8 \\ \hline 22 \end{array}$
3. $\begin{array}{r} 15 \\ +8 \\ \hline 23 \end{array}$
4. $\begin{array}{r} 15 \\ +6 \\ \hline 21 \end{array}$
5. $\begin{array}{r} 13 \\ +9 \\ \hline 22 \end{array}$

6. $\begin{array}{r} 17 \\ +4 \\ \hline 21 \end{array}$
7. $\begin{array}{r} 19 \\ +7 \\ \hline 26 \end{array}$
8. $\begin{array}{r} 16 \\ +5 \\ \hline 21 \end{array}$
9. $\begin{array}{r} 14 \\ +9 \\ \hline 23 \end{array}$
10. $\begin{array}{r} 18 \\ +6 \\ \hline 24 \end{array}$

11. $\begin{array}{r} 12 \\ +8 \\ \hline 20 \end{array}$
12. $\begin{array}{r} 17 \\ +6 \\ \hline 23 \end{array}$
13. $\begin{array}{r} 15 \\ +7 \\ \hline 22 \end{array}$
14. $\begin{array}{r} 13 \\ +7 \\ \hline 20 \end{array}$
15. $\begin{array}{r} 16 \\ +6 \\ \hline 22 \end{array}$

CD-104317 • © Carson-Dellosa   87

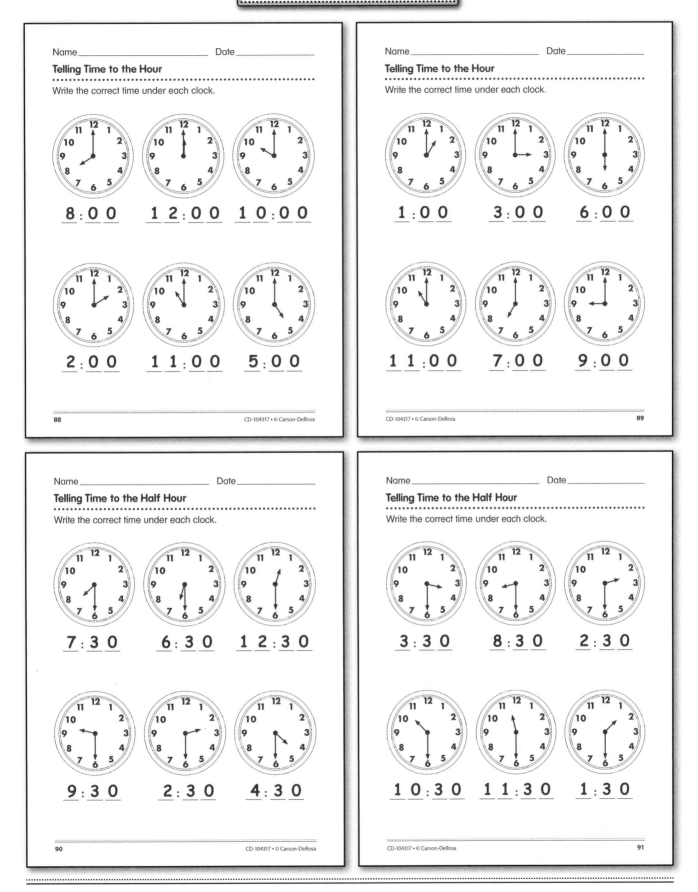

Name_____ Date_____

Telling Time to the Hour

Write the correct time under each clock.

8:00   12:00   10:00

2:00   11:00   5:00

88   CD-104317 • © Carson-Dellosa

Name_____ Date_____

Telling Time to the Hour

Write the correct time under each clock.

1:00   3:00   6:00

11:00   7:00   9:00

CD-104317 • © Carson-Dellosa   89

Name_____ Date_____

Telling Time to the Half Hour

Write the correct time under each clock.

7:30   6:30   12:30

9:30   2:30   4:30

90   CD-104317 • © Carson-Dellosa

Name_____ Date_____

Telling Time to the Half Hour

Write the correct time under each clock.

3:30   8:30   2:30

10:30   11:30   1:30

CD-104317 • © Carson-Dellosa   91

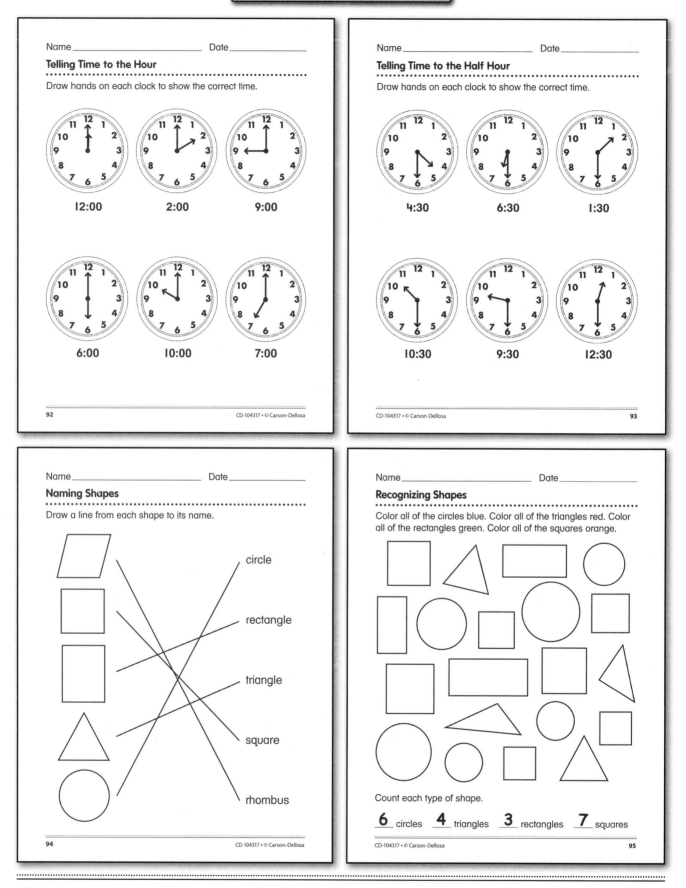

Name_____ Date_____

Telling Time to the Hour

Draw hands on each clock to show the correct time.

12:00   2:00   9:00

6:00   10:00   7:00

92   CD-104317 • © Carson-Dellosa

Name_____ Date_____

Telling Time to the Half Hour

Draw hands on each clock to show the correct time.

4:30   6:30   1:30

10:30   9:30   12:30

CD-104317 • © Carson-Dellosa   93

Name_____ Date_____

Naming Shapes

Draw a line from each shape to its name.

circle

rectangle

triangle

square

rhombus

94   CD-104317 • © Carson-Dellosa

Name_____ Date_____

Recognizing Shapes

Color all of the circles blue. Color all of the triangles red. Color all of the rectangles green. Color all of the squares orange.

Count each type of shape.

6 circles   **4** triangles   **3** rectangles   **7** squares

CD-104317 • © Carson-Dellosa   95

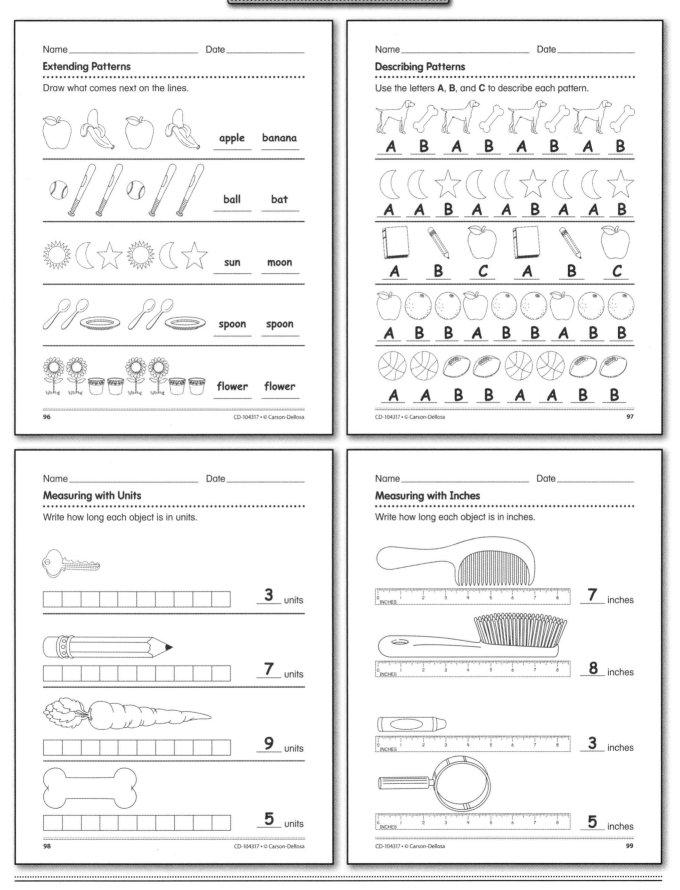

Name _____ Date _____

Extending Patterns

Draw what comes next on the lines.

apple   banana

ball   bat

sun   moon

spoon   spoon

flower   flower

96   CD-104317 • © Carson-Dellosa

Name _____ Date _____

Describing Patterns

Use the letters **A**, **B**, and **C** to describe each pattern.

A B A B A B A B

A A B A A B A A B

A B C A B C

A B B A B B A B B

A A B B A A B B

CD-104317 • © Carson-Dellosa   97

Name _____ Date _____

Measuring with Units

Write how long each object is in units.

3 units

7 units

9 units

5 units

98   CD-104317 • © Carson-Dellosa

Name _____ Date _____

Measuring with Inches

Write how long each object is in inches.

7 inches

8 inches

3 inches

5 inches

CD-104317 • © Carson-Dellosa   99

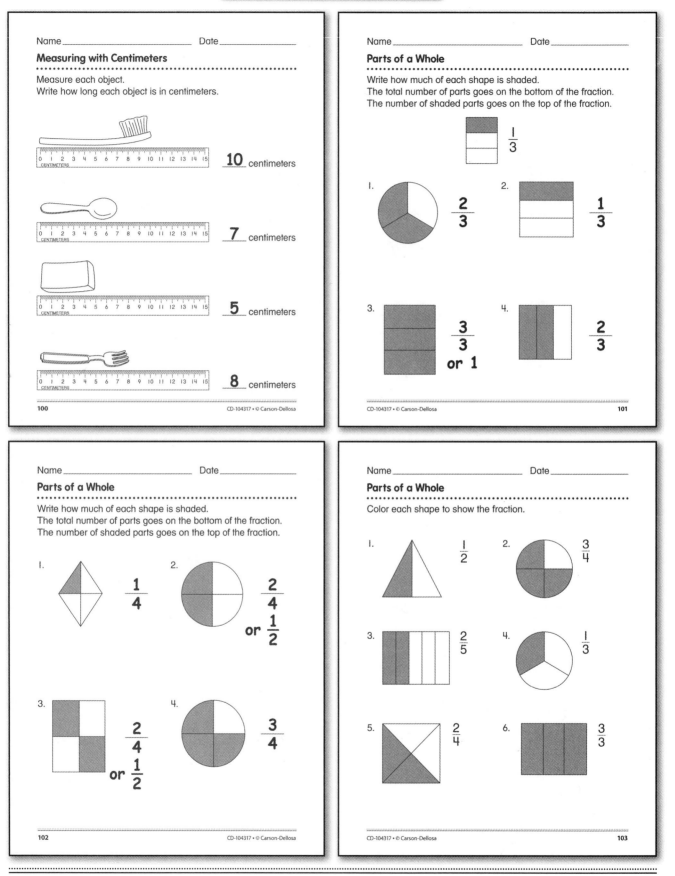

Name_____ Date_____

Measuring with Centimeters
. . . .
Measure each object.
Write how long each object is in centimeters.

10 centimeters

7 centimeters

5 centimeters

8 centimeters

100   CD-104317 • © Carson-Dellosa

Name_____ Date_____

Parts of a Whole
. . . .
Write how much of each shape is shaded.
The total number of parts goes on the bottom of the fraction.
The number of shaded parts goes on the top of the fraction.

$\frac{1}{3}$

1. $\frac{2}{3}$ 2. $\frac{1}{3}$

3. $\frac{3}{3}$ or 1   4. $\frac{2}{3}$

CD-104317 • © Carson-Dellosa   101

Name_____ Date_____

Parts of a Whole
. . . .
Write how much of each shape is shaded.
The total number of parts goes on the bottom of the fraction.
The number of shaded parts goes on the top of the fraction.

1. $\frac{1}{4}$ 2. $\frac{2}{4}$ or $\frac{1}{2}$

3. $\frac{2}{4}$ or $\frac{1}{2}$ 4. $\frac{3}{4}$

102   CD-104317 • © Carson-Dellosa

Name_____ Date_____

Parts of a Whole
. . . .
Color each shape to show the fraction.

1. $\frac{1}{2}$ 2. $\frac{3}{4}$

3. $\frac{2}{5}$ 4. $\frac{1}{3}$

5. $\frac{2}{4}$ 6. $\frac{3}{3}$

CD-104317 • © Carson-Dellosa   103

Congratulations!

receives this award for

_____

_____

Signed _____

Date _____

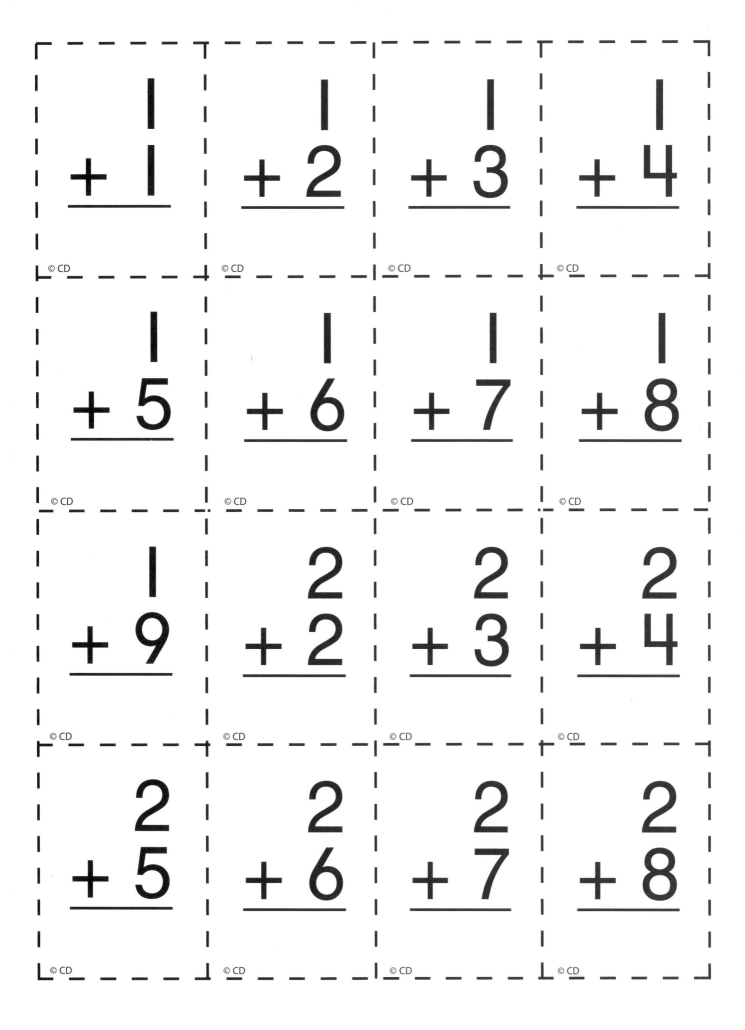

1 + 1	1 + 2	1 + 3	1 + 4
1 + 5	1 + 6	1 + 7	1 + 8
1 + 9	2 + 2	2 + 3	2 + 4
2 + 5	2 + 6	2 + 7	2 + 8

2 + 9	3 + 3	3 + 4	3 + 5
3 + 6	3 + 7	3 + 8	3 + 9
4 + 4	4 + 5	4 + 6	4 + 7
4 + 8	4 + 9	5 + 5	5 + 6

5 + 7	5 + 8	5 + 9	6 + 6
6 + 7	6 + 8	6 + 9	7 + 7
7 + 8	7 + 9	8 + 8	8 + 9
9 + 9	1 − 1	2 − 2	2 − 1

12	14	13	12
14	15	14	13
17	16	16	15
1	0	0	18

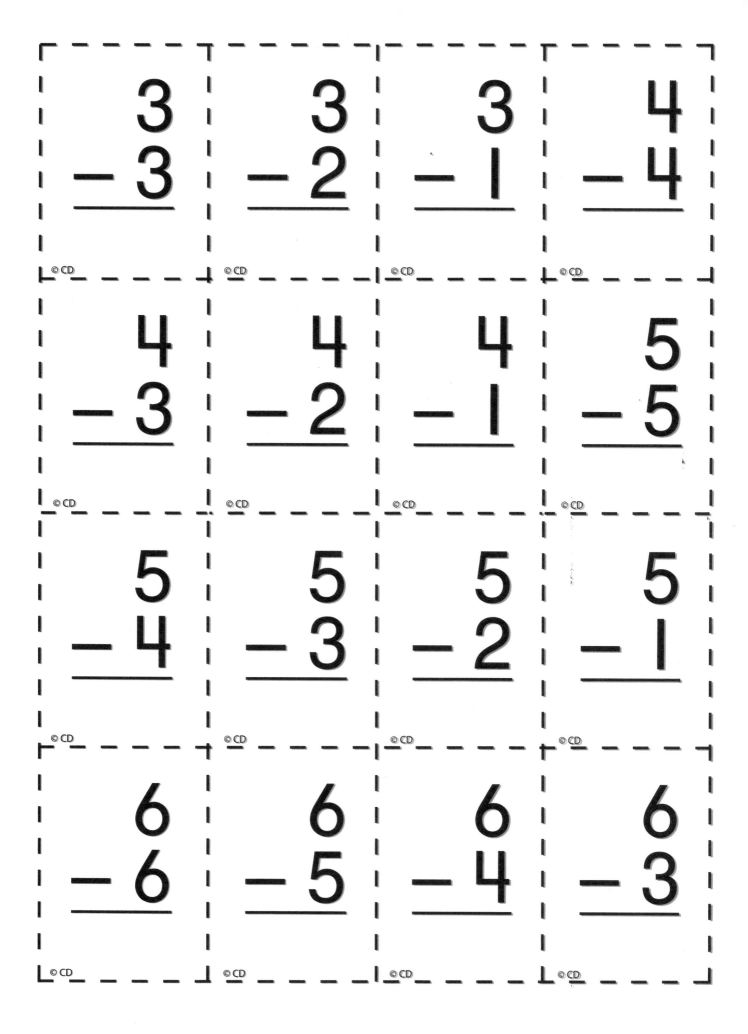

0   2   1   0

0   3   2   1

4   3   2   1

3   2   1   0

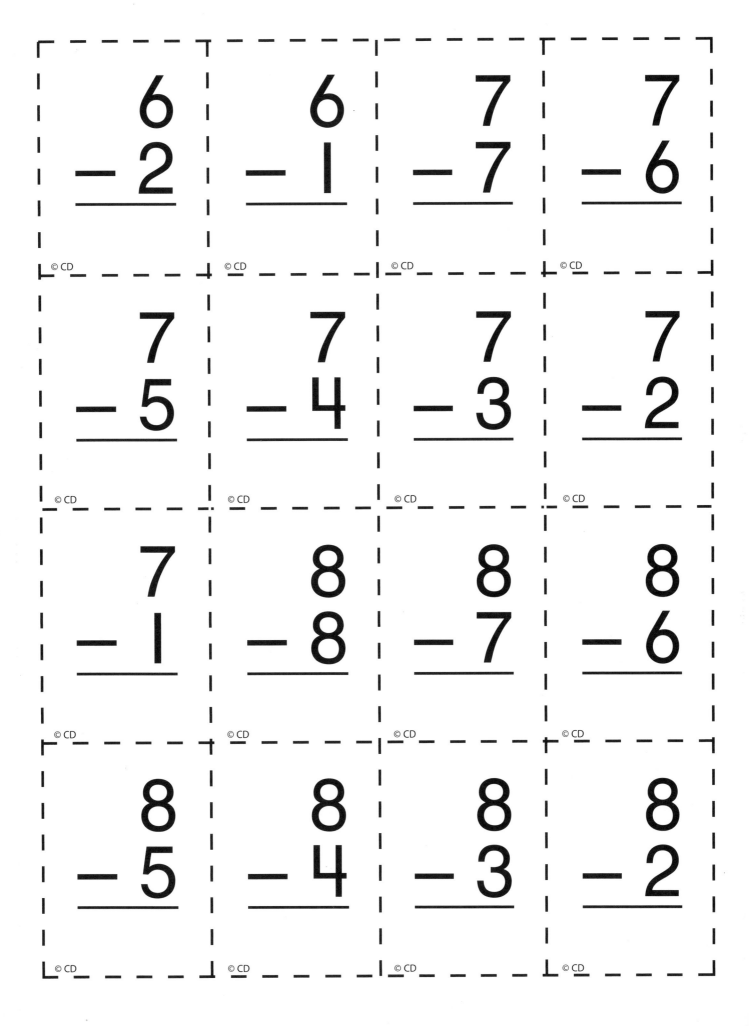

6 − 2	6 − 1	7 − 7	7 − 6
7 − 5	7 − 4	7 − 3	7 − 2
7 − 1	8 − 8	8 − 7	8 − 6
8 − 5	8 − 4	8 − 3	8 − 2

© CD

$\begin{array}{r} 8 \\ -\ 1 \\ \hline \end{array}$	$\begin{array}{r} 9 \\ -\ 9 \\ \hline \end{array}$	$\begin{array}{r} 9 \\ -\ 8 \\ \hline \end{array}$	$\begin{array}{r} 9 \\ -\ 7 \\ \hline \end{array}$

$\begin{array}{r} 9 \\ -\ 6 \\ \hline \end{array}$	$\begin{array}{r} 9 \\ -\ 5 \\ \hline \end{array}$	$\begin{array}{r} 9 \\ -\ 4 \\ \hline \end{array}$	$\begin{array}{r} 9 \\ -\ 3 \\ \hline \end{array}$

$\begin{array}{r} 9 \\ -\ 2 \\ \hline \end{array}$	$\begin{array}{r} 9 \\ -\ 1 \\ \hline \end{array}$	$\begin{array}{r} 10 \\ -\ 0 \\ \hline \end{array}$	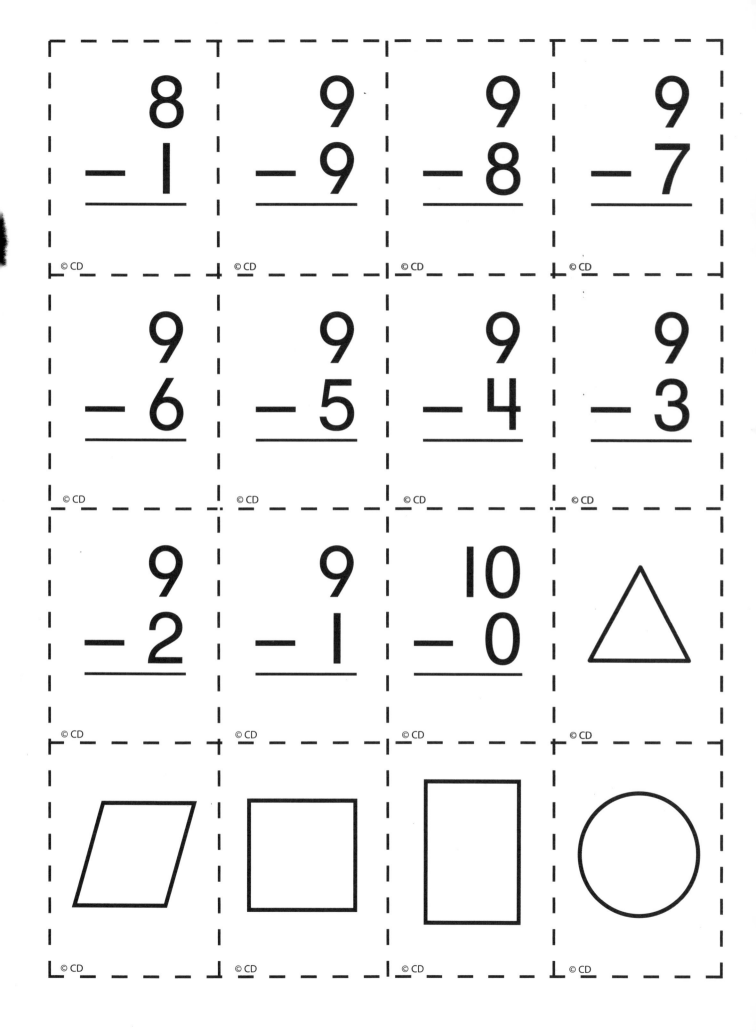

| 2 | I | 0 | 7 |

| <u>6</u> | 5 | 4 | 3 |

triangle | IO | 8 | 7

circle   rectangle   square   rhombus